This book is not intended to provide personalised legal, financial or investment advice. The author and the publisher specifically disclaim any liability, loss or risk that is incurred as a consequence, directly or indirectly, of the use and application of any contents of this work.

Cover design: Tom O'Ryan, JC Social Media
Copyright: © 2020 JayBee Media Limited

The right of Jodie Cook to be identified as the author of this work has been asserted in accordance with the Copyright Designs and Patents Act 1988.

STOP ACTING LIKE YOU'RE GOING TO LIVE FOREVER

36 articles to help you think differently and achieve your version of success, now.

Articles

Introduction

You might be crazy to start a business. You might be crazy not to.

Choosing to start a business means betting everything you have on yourself and your ability to make it a success. But setting up is the easy part.

Running a business is a different story. Maybe it will all go exactly to plan, maybe it won't. Maybe there will be more highs than lows or maybe you'll question why you ever started. This isn't about wishing for a smooth-sailing journey, this is about equipping yourself with the strength and confidence to thrive no matter what is thrown at you. Because that's how the best operate.

Winning sales, losing sales, hiring, firing, growing, stalling. All involve decisions that are yours to make. But what about when it doesn't feel like a choice? How do you sustain your drive and keep going?

What most people don't realise is that lows: challenges, unforeseen circumstances and adverse occurrences, don't have to be lows. It's a matter of opinion, and only yours counts. Someone else's opinion isn't a truth. You can choose what you let in and what you let shape your journey. You only need to be open to the possibility that every possibility is open.

Thoughts, attitudes and beliefs count more than you might realise. So choose to think differently. As Joe Dispenza, author of You Are the Placebo: Making Your Mind Matter, said:

"If you think and feel a certain way, you begin to create an attitude. An attitude is a cycle of short-term thoughts and feelings experienced over and over again. Attitudes are shortened states of being. If you string a series of attitudes together, you create a belief. Beliefs are more elongated states of being and tend to become subconscious. When you add beliefs together, you create a perception. Your perceptions have everything to do with the choices you make, the behaviours you exhibit, the relationships you chose, and the realities you create."

These articles have been written to help you create the reality that matches your personal version of success. They are here to challenge your thinking, show you a different way, or perhaps confirm what you already suspected. They can serve as your personal hype playbook or be there to remind and reassure you that others have faced the challenges you're working through right now.

Perhaps you picked up this book because you suspect you already think differently. Perhaps you're spot-on. You might have a sneaking suspicion that there's more to running a business than being a stressed-out busybody. You might be on the way to creating a life and a career that you love to live. You might be considering taking the leap, absolutely smashing it or stuck in a rut. Either way, welcome.

Jodie Cook, 2020

Stop Acting Like You're Going To Live Forever

Everyone knows someone who always appears to be frantically busy. Too busy sweating the small stuff. Too busy to take on new opportunities. Too busy to enjoy themselves.

"Busy" is not an indicator of success. "Busy" means ineffective time-management or poor prioritisation.

The attitude of "it will be okay in the end" or "I can do that next week" or "next year I'll try that" just won't cut it for serious success. There might not even be a next year! What makes you think you'll be lucky enough to be granted next year?

There's always a way of earning or borrowing more money, hiring more people, or acquiring more information. Time, however, is our only finite resource. Once time is lost it is never found. Don't undervalue your time.

Derek Sivers thinks of his time as being worth $500 an hour, to ensure he is always doing things that are truly worth the outlay. An otherwise very smart business owner I know drives 30 minutes to the gym for £10-a-month cheaper membership than the gym up his road. That's an hour of driving, four times a week, to save a tenner a month. What does that make his hourly rate?!

Authors including Tim Ferriss (4-Hour Work Week), Graham Allcott (Productivity Ninja) and Greg McKeown

(Essentialism) discuss eliminating the unnecessary in order to focus on the absolute essential. Not only that, but focusing on those things that you and you alone can do. In Doctor Meg Jay's TED talk, Why 30 Is Not The New 20, she shares the importance of not seeing your 20s as practice for your 30s. Not wasting time.

Sustainable progression comes from having a sweet balance between urgency and contentment. Relentlessly ambitious whilst also being able to appreciate what you have.

Many successful people in business are big advocates of delegation, automation and elimination. The Tim Ferriss rule for this is: don't delegate anything you can automate; don't automate anything you can eliminate. Don't waste your time, business or otherwise, doing anything that you don't need to do or don't want to do. Because enjoyment matters too. As Gary Vaynerchuk put it in his 2008 TED talk, "You can lose just as much money being happy as hell". Put processes in place to take decision-making or emotions out of standard practices. You can't scale if you're taking everything case-by-case.

This week, whilst staying in central London, I left my laptop charger at my friend's house in an outer suburb. I had three options: Find an Apple store and buy a new one, make the 90-minute round trip to collect it from her, or call a taxi to pick it up and bring it to me. It was a £23 mistake that I'll never make again, but the latter option was the clear winner because it didn't involve me wasting time. Time I knew I could never get back.

How would you run your business if you knew you only had five years to live? What about one year?

Stop idly scrolling Facebook. Stop watching trashy TV. Stop worrying what anyone else thinks. Stop asking pointless questions. Stop having meetings about meetings. Stop doing the 50% of your business tasks that are not fundamental to its success. Use that time to develop yourself or spend more time on the top 10% of actions that will grow your business. Find the balance between contentment and ambition. You are not going to live forever.

"In exactly the same environment, those with a positive mind-set tend to create positive situations, while those with a negative mind-set tend to create negative situations."

Dr Joe Dispenza

The Simple Equation For A Happy Business

It is: **me + you** vs. **the problem.**

Never "me versus you" or "us versus them"

This concept, by author Steve Maraboli, exists to help his readers improve their relationships. It's just as applicable in work as in love. Being on the same team as your employees, your clients, your suppliers and your prospects makes for a happy business.

You are working *with* your employees; to ensure they have a career they love. You're working alongside them so they can become skilled, confident and competent individuals, for the benefit of everyone.

You are working *with* your clients; to grow their business or help them best serve their customers. Their success is your success, their challenges are yours. Share in them and solve them together.

You are working *with* your customers; to improve their lives with the purchase they have made from you. Their concerns are your concerns. Their best interests are your best interests.

You are working *with* your suppliers; so they can best understand your needs and build a long-term relationship with you. Their weaknesses become yours too.

You are even working *with* your competitors; to validate your industry and to uphold the standards of your shared profession. You have more in common with them than you think.

Rarely in business must something be a zero sum game with a winner and a loser. In most situations there is an opportunity to position yourself as being on the same team as the other person and you'll always be pleased you did.

"People don't want to be happy because they think it means giving up on achieving more. More people don't want to believe it's a choice because that puts responsibility in their hands."

Brianna Wiest

How
To
Run A
Business
Without
It
Running
You

If done right, running a business is the best thing in the world. You choose who you work with, you deliver great work you believe in. You set your working times, your values and ethos and you have a career on your own terms. You pre-empt problems and you create a great place to be for everyone involved. Life is a dream.

If done wrong, it's the worst way to operate. You're at the mercy of clients, team members, shareholders and your emails. Instead of being wonderfully in control of processes, you're left fighting fires and backtracking, feeling like you're frantically spinning multiple plates. You've created a prison and you're being held hostage inside it.

The two scenarios described aren't that far apart. Here are the elements that can mean you always experience the former.

Set the rules:

You cannot scale a business if you're taking everything case by case. Offering too many options, every decision needing a multi-person discussion and making concessions and exceptions every day are all recipes for a slow-moving and clunky establishment. It also means you'll be pulled into every scenario, because people need guidance in grey areas.

Commit to communicating the right information, to the right people, at the right time. Make it OK for your team to do the same. Don't answer the same question twice. Nearly all those you answer will have been answered before. Update an FAQ document every time you answer a question and ask your team to as well. Soon you'll have every process mapped out for easy reference and your team will be empowered to use their own reasoned choice.

Know the vision:

Do you know what you stand for and what your business is there to do? Do you know not only your long-term goals, but also what you're going to do in the short term to make sure you achieve them?

If you and your team know the overriding purpose of your existence, short-term decisions should be simple. If you're flitting between multiple visions and agendas then you'll be left confused and so will those you're working with.

Leave no room for misunderstanding. Define and communicate your purpose at every opportunity, and use it as a framework from which everyone operates.

Hire the right people:

If you have a niggling feeling that something's not right, it probably isn't. If you're not 100% convinced about someone in your team, do something about it. When everyone is carrying out their own role in a competent and conscientious way, teams thrive. When there's mistrust, dishonesty or a simply a lack of commercial awareness, everyone loses, especially you as the owner.

The best leaders highlight the work of their team and play down their individual contribution because they know they couldn't operate without them. If you've hired the right people this will be easy to do. If you've hired the wrong people you'll find yourself distancing yourself from them. The latter doesn't lead anywhere good.

Work with people you trust implicitly, who are aligned in their values and operate in a conscientious way. It's the only way everyone can take complete ownership of their own role. As Marcus Aurelius wrote: "What is not good for the beehive, cannot be good for the bees." Everything everyone does needs to be good for the beehive; there can be no selfish agendas.

Put processes in place:

For everything that happens in your business, there is a process that follows. Organisations that run beautifully have action plans mapped out and '"if this then that" documents, all supported by reliable technology that helps founders focus on growing their business and supporting their team. Think of it like Maslow's Hierarchy of Needs, whereby efficient automation and documented processes are the base level that enables the higher stage of creativity and excellence to be accessed.

The default should be that processes run, not that bottlenecks are formed in every department. Sooner or later those bottlenecks will require fire fighting, and that's when you'll be pulled back in. Zoom out, right out, and look at where the breakdowns are happening. Maybe it's hiring, or quality control, or just overflowing inboxes. Practical solutions might involve a task management system, an invoice automation tool or even just better email filters.

Processes should work by default and break only occasionally, not the other way around. However small it might seem, if it's causing a breakdown, it's costing time and attention and must be solved and eliminated.

Address your mindset:

The difference between you running your business and your business running you might be the boundaries you set for yourself. When's the last time you didn't check your email until 10am? Or left a colleague to deliver without micromanaging? How much do you take things personally?

Remind yourself that you have made the choice to run a business. No one forced you to do it. If you're running a successful and growing company with happy clients and a dream team of colleagues, but you still feel like your business runs your life, the problem might exist solely in your mind. Develop other interests, give yourself space and don't be so hard on yourself. If you're actually in a cushy situation but you're telling yourself it's a chore, recognise that you could, instead, choose to chill out and be grateful.

Incorporate balance into your week. If you spend Saturday morning responding to emails, spend Wednesday afternoon taking a walk.

The reason you started a business in the first place was to operate on your own terms, right? So don't take the worst parts of self-employment without allowing yourself the perks. Businesses that run like clockwork without the owner being frazzled do exist, and yours can be one of them!

"Be careful with the labels you use for yourself and others. Those are the masks of your reality."

Tim Ferriss

How To Stop Caring About What Everyone Else Thinks

You exist as a different person in the minds of everyone you have met. No matter what you say or do, others will make judgments and form a unique opinion or mental picture of you as a human being.

Following this logic, there are some personal policies that I follow. One is to never judge someone by someone else's opinion of them. Imagine hearing someone described by another, then meeting them for yourself and realising they are nothing like the portrayal you were led to believe. There are two sides to every story. There's a different perception of every person depending on who offers it. Preconceived beliefs cloud every opinion; they are rarely unbiased.

If someone is talking negatively about you behind your back and it's all stuff that you could dispel if it was said directly to you, then let it go. It's not worth your time; they're not worth your time. As Gary Vaynerchuk said, "I put zero weight into anyone else's opinion of me because I know exactly who I am. Can you say the same?"

Don't have the conversations in your head, don't imagine what you'd say if you saw them. Don't think about them at all. If someone has got you that wrong, if someone is telling themself a narrative that involves you, that just isn't true, let them. Rise above it and let it slide. You can be their obsession, but they'll never be yours.

Make it your personal policy to not say anything behind someone's back you wouldn't say to their face. Think of all those people you know who love to gossip and speak negatively about others when they can't hear. Don't be fooled into thinking you're exempt from this treatment. Consider that they love the drama and love to spread rumours and negativity.

They might have a point to prove, feel they were wronged in some way, or they're simply not that happy in themselves. In any case, it's not your problem. Truly happy people don't need to put others down.

You don't have room for toxicity in your life. Don't join in; just walk away. You don't want to be known as someone who talks about people behind their back. You don't want to lose trust from those you value. If you absolutely have to talk about others when they're not there, say positive things! Be the beacon of positivity and shine brighter than the haters.

So, given that you know everyone you meet will have a different perception of you, how do you make each person's perception favourable? How do you make everyone like you?

Well, you don't. Because it's impossible. It's a waste of your time, too. Show me someone *everyone* likes and understands; let's bet they haven't made much of an impact.

Consider what is in your control and what's out of it. Out: someone else's opinion. In: your own actions. So if your actions are sound, if upon questioning you could reasonably explain every decision you've ever made, let it all go. Why do you care what people think? In the words of Jurgen Klinnsman, football manager, "I'm not here to be liked, I'm here to do a good job".

It's easy to criticise. It's easy to give an opinion. Everyone's got something to say. It's easy for anyone to think they know best. It's easy to judge someone else as inferior, or stupid, or thoughtless. It's easy for someone to think that if they were in your shoes they could do a better job. But the truth is, only you are living your life and only your opinion on it counts.

If someone is talking about you behind your back, it means they're spending time and brain space thinking about you before relaying it to someone else, who then is spending time on you. What a waste of life. Someone who might be insignificant to you is spending their life thinking and talking about you. All things considered, it's rather flattering.

Let anyone else think anything they like. Who cares? There were never any statues erected to celebrate critics. Those who cannot should not stand in the way of those who can. Ronnie Coleman said, "Everybody wants to be a bodybuilder, but nobody wants to lift no heavy-ass weights." Lions do not lose sleep over the opinions of sheep.

It's easy to criticise others but it's not easy to do everything perfectly yourself, especially when you have plans bigger than most people could even imagine. It's not easy to be such a winner. You know that.

You don't need everyone's approval and you certainly don't need everyone to like you. For everything worthwhile you do there will be countless people who would have done it differently. But who cares, right? This isn't your first rodeo. You know what you're doing. Play the long game. Rise above it all and refuse to engage. Let it slide. Stop losing sleep over the opinions of sheep and don't be sidetracked by people who are not on track themselves.

"Our overnight success took 1000 days."

Brian Chesky, Airbnb founder

The Greek Word To Live Your Life By

Believing in yourself and knowing your goals is paramount to your success and happiness. However, as TV shows and our social media feeds become awash with big houses, flashy cars and people seemingly earning thousands of dollars a day, it's easy to become disheartened and distracted and start questioning your life decisions.

A word I remember every day is *euthymia*. In Seneca's essays on tranquillity, he defines euthymia as "believing in yourself and trusting you are on the right path, and not being in doubt by following the myriad footpaths of those wandering in every direction." This old Greek word has an incredibly powerful and important application for modern living.

To me, in practice, euthymia is the difference between calm and frantic, patience and rushing, present and expectant. It's what allows me to be solid rather than malleable, content rather than envious.

Diogenes Laërtuis describes euthymia as, "Cheerfulness, a condition according to which the soul lives calmly and steadily, being disturbed by no fear, or superstition, or other passion." It's also a word used to describe a stable, middle state in those diagnosed with bipolar disorder.

Here's why I believe the word euthymia and its application to work and life has never been more relevant and important:

Social media and comparisons

Whilst we're scrolling a stranger's Instagram feed and gathering a snapshot of how they spend their time, it's easy to feel pangs of envy and begin to compare our own reality with their feed. Over time it can wear away at our self-esteem and self worth and contribute to mental health problems regarding identity and purpose. More importantly, someone's social media portrays *their* version of success, not necessarily ours. Will this lead to us thinking we want what they have, when we actually don't?

I believe that keeping the concept of euthymia at the forefront of your mind helps avoid those pitfalls. If you clearly know your own path and purpose, you simply won't have feelings of envy towards anyone else's life. Even beyond that; if you know what you're trying to achieve you probably aren't spending that much time scrolling the social media profiles of other people; you're working on your own game.

How do you avoid following the myriad footpaths of those wandering in every direction? You know your own path and you stick to it.

Alice: Would you tell me, please, which way I ought to go from here?

The Cheshire Cat: That depends a good deal on where you want to get to.

Alice: I don't much care where.

The Cheshire Cat: Then it doesn't much matter which way you go.

- Alice in Wonderland

Internet and opportunity

Thanks to internet access and online platforms such as eBay, Amazon, Shopify and Wordpress, it's straightforward for nearly anyone to pick up a laptop, watch a few tutorials and start a business. Anyone who has done it knows that starting is easy; it's turning that start into a long-term success that's not.

Marketing campaigns aimed at business owners or startups don't want you to think it's going to be demanding, or hard work. The rhetoric is instant gratification and quick wins; mistaking years of hard work for an overnight success, perhaps because it's more accessible and will more likely lead to sales of their product. As professionals, of course we want to believe that we are only days away from success. From winning the lottery or someone finally discovering us. The internet makes that all possible... right?

Actually, promises of quick wins, lottery mind-sets, and opportunities that seem too good to be true are exactly that. A distraction and a detour designed to benefit someone else by misleading you.

If you're not sure of your own path or where you're going, you could be fooled into thinking that success via an alternative method is easier, or that there's a quick-win to be seized. There are no quick wins. There is no silver bullet. You make it easier by putting the work in and laying solid foundations to build on, not by flitting about believing every sales video advertised to you.

Remember Tom from MySpace? He could have raised millions in investment and turned MySpace into today's Facebook. He could be attending conferences with world leaders and giving keynote speeches. He could be ploughing the profits into space travel and working out how to colonise other planets. But Tom from MySpace didn't want to do that. He knew his own path and nothing could deter him from that. Tom sold MySpace in 2009 for $580 million and has since been travelling the world taking photographs.

Perspective and opinions

In 2014 Oprah Winfrey published a book called What I Know For Sure. It follows her journey, her experience and how she finds the truths she can believe in. Then she lives according to these truths. For everything you believe to be true, there will be someone who believes it to be untrue. Euthymia says this doesn't matter. As long as you have defined your own beliefs about the world around you and your place within it, you can hear other perspectives and opinions, take them on board, but let them slide off you rather than infiltrate your core.

Once you have defined what you do and don't believe to be true, and set your own goals for life and work, be careful about sharing them. In the 2010 TED talk by Derek Sivers, he urges you to "Keep your goals to yourself". According to the talk, sharing your goals makes you feel like you've already achieved them.

I believe that sharing your goals allows others to tell you why you might not achieve them; which might deter you from your path. Euthymia says be sure of your own goals and how you'll get there, but focus on quietly working away instead of shouting loudly.

"You're braver than you believe, stronger than you seem and smarter than you think."

- Winnie the Pooh

In Ichiro Kishimi's book, The Courage To Be Happy, he says, "Don't be afraid of other people looking at you, don't pay attention to other people's judgment and don't seek recognition from other people. Just choose the path that is best for you and that you believe in." Euthymia reminds me to choose the advice I take on board and the opinions I value.

Define your happy, your goals and your truths and stay on your own path. Euthymia.

"You're never too important to be nice to people."

Jason Graystone

Cruelty
Is
Weakness
And
Everyone
Knows
It

The happy person writes positive reviews, offers the benefit of the doubt, gives constructive criticism in private, and can see the other side of the story. The happy person serves to lift, elevate and inspire others, not complain and moan as one of life's victims.

Truly happy, secure, and confident people do not put others down, gossip, or defame. They don't need to. They are too busy focusing on their own game and they will continue to do so. They refuse to respond, comment, or even acknowledge the presence of naysayers or jealous onlookers.

In a world of shocking news headlines and sensationalism, you might think that everything is there for you to comment on. But it's not. From Twitter users tweeting artists to tell them their work is rubbish, someone leaving a 1 star review of Scottish mountain Ben Nevis, to internet trolls and the gossipers who just can't keep a dignified silence; showing cruelty, externalising negative opinions, or allowing yourself to form them in the first place is a recipe for unhappiness.

All cruelty stems from weakness. This applies every time you make a snide remark or cruel comment or do something in an attempt to defame. Those actions stem from insecurity or guilt. No mean comment ever made anyone look stronger, and I feel sorry for those who feel like they can only rise up by putting others down.

How you see the world is a reflection of your own strengths, weaknesses, talents and shortcomings. The pessimist, the cynic, and the no-hoper will experience a different reality than the chilled out, joy-spreading optimist.

Happy people see others as equals and develop empathy towards teammates. Strong individuals let things slide. Confident beings rise above the drama, believe their own truths and refuse to be dragged down. It only serves to infuriate, but they don't mind that. They will rise, again and again, in superhero-like fashion and a way that seems unattainable to haters.

Choose your thoughts, actions and words carefully. Positive or negative? Optimist or pessimist? Radiator or drainer? Pick a side, because it will define you.

"Sometimes people let the same problem make them miserable for years when they could just say "so what". That's one of my favourite things to say."

Andy Warhol

Five Things To Cut Out Of Your Conversations

Meeting people, getting to know them and building your tribe involves the art of conversation. Getting good at conversation leads to meaningful relationships and leaving others with a positive lasting impression. According to Charlie Tremendous Jones, "You will be the same person in five years as you are today except for the people you meet and the books you read."

If you've ever left a conversation feeling underwhelmed or perturbed, one of these five things could be behind it. Avoid creating that feeing in others by cutting the following out:

One-upping

Your business is going well but the person you're speaking with knows someone who's absolutely smashing it. We've all been in those kind of conversations and they never have the desired effect. Let others have their moment and be supportive and encouraging instead of feeling like you have to one-up. Your time will come, so stay humble and resist the urge to get involved. Onlookers can see right through it, anyway.

Discovery ownership

So you read the 4-Hour Work Week way before anyone else. Congratulations. Maybe you were vegan before it was cool. Or discovered Stoicism in high school. If you were ahead of the curve in any way, it really isn't important and you don't need everyone to know.

As Ricky Maye said, "Conversation isn't about proving a point; true conversation is about going on a journey with the people you are speaking with."

What matters is that you are acting true to yourself and you are happy and willing to share your experience with others if they should ask for it. Who cares if someone thinks you're on the bandwagon? If something has changed your life for the better, let that be enough.

Boxing in

Guessing someone's thoughts or actions based on labels you have administered is a dangerous game that no one takes kindly to. Appreciate that how you see someone might not be how they see themselves, so it's always better to ask and understand rather than assume or label.

If you've ever been categorised or put in a box by someone else, you'll know how frustrating it can be and how wrong they can have you!

Putting down

Not all punch lines need to come at the expense of others. It's possible, and desirable, to be funny without insulting anyone else. In the 48 Laws of Power, Robert Greene advises, "Never joke about appearances or taste", two matters he deems highly sensitive to others. See others as equals and talk to them as such. Someone insulting your appearance or taste is a sign of their weakness, not yours.

As Dorothy Nevill said, "The real art of conversation is not only to say the right thing at the right place but to leave unsaid the wrong thing at the tempting moment." Think before you speak to consider how it might be received!

Phubbing

When you're talking to someone, give them your full attention. Avoid looking for opportunities to get your phone out. Chatting whilst scrolling just sends the message that what someone else is saying isn't as important as what might be happening on the internet at any given moment. "Phubbing", phone-snubbing, is real and it's costing human interaction and genuine connection. Don't be that guy. Someone I know just walks away if the person he's engaging with gets out their phone. He gives his full attention and expects the same in return.

As author Samuel Johnson said, "The happiest conversation is that of which nothing is distinctly remembered, but a general effect of pleasing impression." Doing anything other than fully listening, sharing stories and asking great follow-up questions is missing the point of conversation. Avoid one-upmanship, being precious, delivering put-downs and phubbing to have conversations that leave a lasting positive impression and relationships that thrive.

"To be successful in life you need a funnybone, a wishbone and a backbone."

Sign on the wall, Bird Rock Coffee, San Diego

Eight Ways To Have Better Relationships With Your Clients

If you're providing a service of any sort, you will have clients. Your client relationships; the presence, happiness and retention of them; are the foundation of your business. Your company exists to serve its clients and their needs and without them you don't have a business.

When you're faced with a looming deadline or an unreasonable request, it's easy to wish for a simpler role without such demands. Many business owners I know have confided that they are sure there are easier ways of making a living than having clients to answer to.

That's completely the wrong way to think about it. The truth is, learning to be exceptional at understanding and looking after your clients means you can have the best of all worlds. It means you get to work with people you admire, who look forward to hearing from you, with whom you work in partnership, for mutual benefit. Being paid to do work you love is how you win at life.

From 15 years of experience in client relations and customer service, here's what I've learned on how to do it best:

Make a great first impression

From the moment your client commits to working with you, you have a small window of opportunity in which to make a great impression and set the relationship up for success. Loyalty and trust have to be earned, they don't come automatically. Assume you are starting at zero and be hungry to prove your value and make them confident they made the right decision.

Ask your client how they want to communicate, operate based on their version of success and always be exceptional.

Be on the same team

Working in partnership with your client means being on the same team, working for the success of their business, at all times. There is no "us" and "them", there's no competition here. As Marcus Aurelius said, "That which isn't good for the beehive isn't good for the bee." This means sharing problems and solutions without being precious about whose idea was whose because in the bigger picture it doesn't matter.

The more you immerse yourself in their business the more value you can add. The more your vision and ethos is shared the better your client relationships will be.

Become an ideas machine

Operating from the ethos that you are on the same team and working towards shared goals, your client's company is now your own company, so treat it as such. Think about its problems and come up with ideas on how to solve them. At my social media agency, some of the ideas we give our clients have nothing to do with social media. The account manager just understands the needs of their client so much that they can give an alternative, yet very relevant, perspective. This can be invaluable to our clients, not to mention a valid reason for continuing to work with us.

Practice coming up with ideas and share all of them with your client. If they want to present these ideas as their own, be flattered, not offended!

Take an interest

Always be pleased to hear from your client. Don't do this because you feel like you have to, do it because you genuinely care. Take an active interest in their life, work, hopes and dreams and understand how they think about things and make decisions. When they tell you something, write it down and make a note to follow up.

The more you understand and get to know your clients the more you can see the world from their point of view, which in turn helps you do your best work for them.

Take pride in your work

No amount of client relationship building will make up for shoddy workmanship. The first focus should be committing to excellence in the work that your client has commissioned you for. If it's not good enough, don't submit it. If you could do better, keep working until you're proud.

Representing your client's company as if it was your very own means only presenting work that meets your high standards. Make it so good that you're excited to show them.

Make life easy for them

Look for opportunities to take any burden off your client. Send them the Zoom link, prepare the meeting agenda, explain the next steps and take the notes. Follow up your follow-ups and have a calm, proactive and organised influence on any situation in which they involve you.

If you're a nuisance to deal with and you don't do what you say you will, at some point they'll just opt out of working with you. Build a reputation for being a solid and reliable person; one that your client is proud to have on their team.

Over-communicate

Everyone loves to receive a good status update and your client is no different. Regularly send clear outlines of the work you've completed, what you will be working on next, as well as any blockers or action required of your client. The more they understand what you're doing, the more you can work together as a successful team. Exude control and ownership and don't scrimp on sending status updates, even as small FYI or "no response required" memos.

If someone knows that you're beavering away at the tasks in hand, it heightens the sense of camaraderie that you're trying to develop.

Take them seriously

If your client thinks there's a problem, it's up to you to find the solution and communicate it to them. You have two choices here, you can play it down and tell them nothing is wrong, or you can take it seriously and cover all bases in putting it right. Whichever option you choose, your client will choose the other one. "What do you mean this isn't a problem! I need you to look at this urgently!" or "Don't worry so much, I'm probably overreacting, I'm sure it's nothing." Take their concerns seriously and do everything in your power to alleviate them.

Your clients and their satisfaction is the reason your business exists and it's not something to gloss over. Learning to get really good at looking after them will set you both up for success and prosperity.

"If you want to see what you're truly committed to, look at your results."

Jennifer Ho-Dougatz

Two Mantras To Shape Your Year

There are two mantras that I read mid-way through this year that led to the second half of the year being unrecognisable from the first.

Everything flourished. I felt great. I had more energy for my work. My calendar only contained events I was looking forward to going to. Projects were finished promptly and opportunities presented themselves. Doors were opened and I felt like I was living the life I wanted and deserved. I'm telling you them so you can feel that way too.

These aren't mantras I invented, they are ones I read and then couldn't stop thinking about. The fact that they were there, in front of me, felt less of a discovery of something new and more like a confirmation of what I suspected to be true but hadn't managed to put into words myself. They resonated so deeply that I wanted them to be at the forefront of my mind, always. I made them my desktop backgrounds and I wrote them at the top of journal entries.

Mantra one: I am the hero of my own life.

I read this in 101 Essays To Change The Way You Think, by Brianna Wiest. It's also the title of her guided journal.

Asserted by Wiest, is that "How you act in the face of what you can't control determines whether you are the hero or the victim of your own life."

In any given day, a whole host of less-than-ideal occurrences can happen. Adverse news, adverse weather, bad feedback, a misconstrued exchange, anything! Choosing to be the victim, whether deliberately or subconsciously, means complaining, retaliating, whingeing, or doing anything other than making a plan and moving past the obstacle. Everyone has problems. You always will have them. Don't wish for a future where you don't. Instead, build the strength to thrive no matter what is thrown at you.

Choosing to be the hero of your own life means asking the question, "What am I going to do about this now?" instead of wallowing in self-pity or blaming someone else. The mantra reminds me that the decision is in my power and my happiness and success is down to me.

The world is indifferent to your existence, and that's a good thing. It means you can do whatever you want. You can choose to rise above and you can refuse to engage. You can choose to plough on with your own dreams and if they are so big they scare others, well that's even better. Because you are indifferent to the need to be accepted or recognised by anyone other than the person in the mirror who is looking back at you with high hopes and quiet confidence.

Choosing to be the hero of your own life empowers others to choose to be the hero of theirs. You be you, and I'll be me. Make it the default that every thought, word and action you have is deliberate and true to the best version of you that exists.

Mantra two: We are what we repeatedly do.

It's obvious really, isn't it? Yet this quote, by Aristotle, is so often overlooked.

Do you think you can coast and do the bare minimum and still be considered for an opportunity? You can't be a writer without writing, or a singer without singing, or a dancer without dancing. You cannot be excellent unless you practice excellence in everything you do. What you let slide in rehearsal you'll get wrong in the final show. Mistakes in training come out when you're competing. You can't put on an act for anyone because your true colours will show. We are what we repeatedly do.

Repeatedly being late, missing deadlines, practising negativity and doing work you're not proud of will define your existence.

I'm sure there were some jammy exceptions in high school. Those kids who didn't really bother or commit yet still got straight As. But it doesn't happen in the real world, so putting in sub-maximal effort and expecting maximum results is a pipe dream up there with winning the lottery without actually buying a ticket. It's not going to happen.

Committing to showing up, getting your head down, learning, developing, growing and practising excellence is the only way to make it happen consistently. Treat everyone with respect. Proofread all your emails. Turn up on time. Demand excellence from yourself.

Perfect practice makes perfect performance. Developing a reputation for excellence reaps future rewards; it's an exponential curve. Promotions and opportunities aren't offered based on gambles. Those offering them want dead certs, and the best indicator of future performance is past performance rather than words or promises or being "passionate". This is about doing your ability justice rather than proving yourself to anyone else. Intrinsic motivation should be all you need.

Every interaction, conversation, decision or thought you have is a chance to practice being the person you want to be. Repeat. Every single day. From Jim Cathert, "How would the person I want to be do the things I'm about to do?"

"I am the hero of my own life" reminds me that my actions are a choice, and "We are what we repeatedly do" reminds me to consistently make good choices and form habits that yield the results I want.

Once you keep these mantras at the forefront of your every waking moment, you don't waste a seconds' thought or an eon of energy on anything or anyone that isn't fulfilling the mission you have set for yourself.

"If you absolutely can't tolerate critics, then don't do anything new or interesting."

Jeff Bezos

Read
This
And
They
Will
Never
Break
You

They will try. They will say things. They will do things. On purpose and by accident. But they will never break you. They will antagonise, goad, lure you down their path, but you will see straight through it. Their venom, toxicity, it doesn't touch you.

You know, for sure, that you have nothing to prove, no one to answer to, no words you need to use to dignify any attack with an answer. You let it all slide because they haven't broken you. Haven't even scratched the surface, haven't made the smallest dent.

Let them try. Let them watch your every move and think of ways to bring you down. They will never succeed. There are those that do and there are those that watch in awe. You will not mistake their insecurity for superiority. They may mistake your kindness for weakness. You are far from broken, far from giving in. In fact, their words only make you stronger. You're ruffling their world and they haven't touched yours. They're putting minutes, hours, days into thinking about you and you have forgotten they exist.

The power is yours. The weakness is theirs. The jealousy is theirs. You see them for who they are and you know it's a shame they miss out on who they could be. Time, energy, brain-space spent watching, obsessing over you. It will never be returned, but they are desperate that it is.

They will create their own demise or they will find their own success. Either is fine, because you are indifferent. You wish them well because you truly don't care. And that's what frustrates them the most. That to such a significant person in their life they are insignificant in return. They had your trust, your time, and they threw it away. Now they will never have your response, your energy, your thoughts. They will never break you. They will never come close.

"Don't over-celebrate the wins. Don't commiserate the losses. They are just things. In the grand scheme of things, with your limited time here on the earth, they don't really matter."

Dan Meredith

Six Things You Need To Get Over To Become A Successful Entrepreneur

What's stopping you fulfilling your potential, preventing you from taking action or slowing your progress as a business owner?

Conditioning your mind for success involves letting these things well and truly slide:

The opinions of naysayers

If you have a plan that you are convinced will work, go for it. If it's true to your values, fits with your vision and you feel good about it, why not? Not everyone will agree with you because they don't know what you are capable of. They don't realise you've already done your research, weighed up the pros and cons and crafted a strategy. You know your audience and only they determine your fate.

Many an entrepreneur has been told that their business idea will never take off. It doesn't mean it's true. Someone airing their doubts about your business is a projection of their reality, not yours. Don't internalise negativity levelled at you and don't let someone else's limited beliefs be yours.

Thinking too small

As Daniel Burnham, architect of Chicago, said, "Make no little plans; they have no magic to stir men's blood and probably themselves will not be realised." Make plans so big they scare you. Make plans so big that thinking about achieving them spurs you into action and motivates you to keep going. The small wins will happen along the way as you consistently put the work in, but it's the big juicy needle-moving accomplishments that make you remarkable.

You don't need to tell everyone your grandiose plans. Just know them yourself and know the steps ahead of achieving them. As Seth Godin said, You're either remarkable or invisible."

Feeling embarrassed

No matter what you're creating or selling, you will, at some point, need to put yourself out there. For your customers to buy into your brand and your story they will need to see it. This is no time to shy away from the limelight for fear of ridicule.

If you have a niggling feeling that something isn't right, work out what it is and fix it. If the only niggling feeling is the adrenalin you get from being centre stage, channel it into action, start taking the steps and find your audience.

Maybe it is embarrassing telling people that you're starting a business, or growing a business, or looking for customers. But who cares? Be shameless. You'd much rather do that than sit in silence and let opportunities pass you by.

Dreams without plans and action

There must be a connection between the dreams you have and the actions you are putting in place. Avoid having dreams that don't link to plans because you will just get frustrated at not achieving them. You might think you want to be fluent in Spanish, but have you signed up to the courses, downloaded the language apps and booked the trip to Madrid? A dream without a plan is just a wish, and wishing is not a strategy for success.

Turning up to an arbitrary desk for eight hours a day to tap away at a keyboard answering emails and going to pointless meetings isn't progress. It's definitely busyness, it's definitely activity, but wasting time in between weekends isn't going to get you to the milestones you have in mind. If you really want to get somewhere, work out the route there and ignore everything else.

Feeling like it's too soon

If your current situation is cushy or if you are daunted by the thought of starting a business, it will never feel like the right time to begin. If you're already running a profitable and stable organisation, it might not ever feel like the right time to think bigger, reinvest or take risks. Sure, you could hang back, take it slower and play golf on weekdays, but you're capable of so much more than that and you'd be doing yourself and the world a disservice to succumb.

The hardest thing is starting. Once you've started, you know the drill and you learn quickly from there. You develop conscious competence, then unconscious competence, and then suddenly you can do the basics excellently without even trying. That's where the real magic happens and that's the time to keep pushing, not the time to back off. Get started now.

Being all talk

In the 2015 film The Big Short, Christian Bale plays Michael Burry, one of the first people to discover the American housing market bubble. When he's working, operating his own hedge fund, he is running through the numbers doing the work that his clients commission him to do, but he ignores nearly all of their calls. He could spend his days gossiping with them or talking vaguely about investing, but he doesn't. He communicates only when he has something important to say. He has something important to say because he's working at it and not looking for excuses not to.

Deep down, you know what you should be doing and how spending your time will add the most value. But there's a difference between saying you want to write a book and actually writing a book. Between launching a brilliant product and just talking about it. Progress, not busyness. Action, not words.

Fear of failure

When starting or scaling a business, things will crop up that you haven't foreseen. It's inevitable. But working out how to move past obstacles, as well as seeing them as fun challenges to be solved, is what separates great entrepreneurs from those who never quite reach their potential.

What's the worst that can happen? It doesn't work out, you have to close down and then you start again. I'd choose that over never starting any day. If you don't view anything as failure then it's not failure. If someone else views it as failure then they have no place in your life. Only your labels for you count. You only fail when you give up.

Get comfortable in that unknown space and don't tie your own success to outcomes you can't control, or winning the support of people who don't have your back. If you need some motivation to see past potential failure, talk to someone who has achieved things you aspire to achieve, make yourself a hype playlist or remind yourself that one day you won't be here and neither will anyone you know.

"Nothing either good or bad, but thinking makes it so."

William Shakespeare

If
In
Doubt,
Choose
Kindness

No matter what you think someone has done, to harm you directly or from lack of care, you can always choose kindness.

You can always be the bigger person; you can always choose to forgive. You can always opt to get on with your life and hope that some day they can get on with theirs.

There's no excuse for trolling, meanness or malicious attacks, ever. You will never understand what someone is going through, and acting out of anything other than kindness shows you don't understand how humans work.

It might be the hardest thing you have to do. To smile and say hi instead of beginning a confrontation. To resist shouting and to resist judgment. To respond with a positive comment instead of a mean jibe. But you have the power within you to do it and you'll always be pleased you did.

As Brianna Wiest said, "How you deal with the things you cannot control determines whether you are the hero or the victim of your life."

To those who believe they are victims: set yourself free. You are feeling this way because you have let it happen. It was no one else's fault, and that's a good thing, because you don't need anyone else to become the hero again either. You can always control your actions and your words and what you do with your voice. Re-build your bridges, choose to forgive, choose to let go. Choose kindness. Not because you want recognition, not because you have a point to prove. Choose kindness because that's all you want on your conscience and your reputation.

Choose kindness because deep down you know it's right. Choose kindness because you're a happy person with lots to offer the world, not a victim.

Meet malice with malice and what happens? The perpetrator is vindicated in their actions. You fought fire with fire and you both lost. Lost your minds, lost your sense of perspective, lost your sense of humanity. You can choose to keep yours when you choose kindness.

"Kindness brings kindness out of others. Take the extra steps to be kind in disagreement and have faith that there is kindness in most all of us. Do whatever is needed to rid yourself of those that constantly show hatred and selfishness."

John Cena

Can Your Business Survive You Going On Holiday?

Two-thirds of business owners check their emails every day whilst on holiday, according to research recently carried out by American Express. Whilst this may sound like a lot, I'd wager that the rest are kidding themselves. Or don't go on holiday. Business owners check their emails every day.

The survey of 2000 business owners running companies with fewer than fifty employees found that 50% said checking work emails while away made them feel happier and more in control of their time. Furthermore, 50% of business owners never set an out of office when they go away.

Understanding these numbers requires an understanding of two words that have changed in meaning.

The word "office" used to describe the place you went to in order to work. Only in your office could you work. Now everywhere can be your office; your home, the train, a coffee shop, even a yurt on a mountainside. For many professions you just need a laptop and an internet connection, making remote working easier than ever.

The word "holiday" used to refer to uninterrupted time away from this office. But since the office has changed in meaning, so has the holiday. It's possible to spend the morning working from an AirBNB in Hawaii before surfing all afternoon. Or climb Cape Town's Table Mountain by day whilst emailing and writing proposals by night. Does that still constitute a holiday? Sure! The lines between work and home are increasingly blurred, and I'm not convinced that's a bad thing.

The research seems to agree. In fact, almost one-in-five business owners said they would not travel somewhere if they knew in advance they would be unable to stay connected. Those who have taken the leap to start and run their own business want to make the most of the benefits it can bring. The ability to work from anywhere in the world is one of them, which can render the term "holiday" out-dated and irrelevant.

It's not a question of business owners putting the work in; it's a question of when they do it. As Robert Frost, American poet, said, "By working faithfully eight hours a day, you may eventually get to be a boss and work twelve hours a day."

Coffee shop owner and friend, Lydia Papaphilippopoulos says, "The trick is to have a team that don't take liberties and try to encroach on your time when you're away on holiday. Make sure they know only to contact you if it's a genuine emergency." she admits that she too checks her emails while away, but that "it doesn't feel like a chore because I love what I do. I might turn off push notifications and take time to myself, sure, but I still have the power to choose how and when I respond."

In another article, I explored whether the concept of work-life balance was overrated, following results of a study that found business owners did not prioritise their own health and wellbeing as much as they prioritised the health and wellbeing of their teams. Is this a similar finding? I encourage everyone in my team to schedule regular holidays, to switch off completely whilst away; to put their out of office on and to not check their emails, safe in the knowledge that all will be taken care of. I choose not to stick to this myself.

The "choice" aspect of this came up in the research, in that 65% of those running their own company say they *choose* to work flexibly and a vast majority of business owners (88%) described the *choice* to work outside of the identified core working hours as a personal one. Perhaps business owners choose to check their emails to make sure nothing has kicked off, to enable them to fully relax. If so, isn't that just part of the role?

I don't like the traditional notion of the term "holiday" entirely because I think it's indicative of the unsustainable boom and bust nature of living that I try to avoid. I don't believe in out of office responders, because I don't think emails should require an instant response anyway. I want to work and relax according to what I'm feeling like at the time. If that involves writing articles and calling clients by a beach, or going to the gym at 11am, or climbing mountains on Thursdays but doing podcast interviews during the evenings, then great. The world is a different place and the confines of 9-5, offices and holidays don't need to apply.

It's been well documented that the way most people work isn't working for them, including extensively by Tony Schwarz in his books and TEDx talk. After reading Schwarz's work, Joel Gascoigne, founder of Buffer, conducted a lifestyle experiment whereby he worked every day of the week for 5 hours, with those hours split across the whole day. He also worked out every day, rested and reflected every day, and wrote up the whole process. He didn't continue with this routine after the experiment, but it gave him insights into how, where and when he did want to work to build his company.

If you're looking to truly switch off ahead of going away in summer, or if you're back from a holiday and frustrated that you didn't switch off when you wanted to, put the steps in place to get it right next time.

This might involve scheduling other, taxing exercises like skiing, mountain biking or water sports so you can't physically check your phone. Perhaps you could disconnect your email and work chat accounts from your phone, or schedule phone-free times such as at meal times. Finally, be honest with yourself: what are you worried about? Does your team need more training to take care of unexpected occurrences? Or do you just need to trust them more? No good team wants their boss to be overworked, so communicate your plans with your colleagues and clients in advance and let them hold you accountable to actually getting some rest!

"When you're running a marathon you don't worry about how sprinters are doing!"

Gary Vaynerchuk

Consumption Is Killing Your Success

Spending hours each week watching the news, scrolling social media and reading opinion pieces is stopping you from creating masterpieces of your own.

The internet has us glued and yearning for new information and fast entertainment. And we are never satiated.

What would happen if for every hundred tweets you read, you wrote one? For every five articles you read you published one of your own? Every hour spent watching YouTube was spent creating tutorials and webinars? Or for every few books you finished reading, you finished writing another of yours?

What if you spent that last hour creating a great article rather than consuming the news or social media? What if rather than being influenced by the things you saw, you were influencing others? Crafting compelling content and making an impact on people is a skill and an art. It has to be practiced and you will get better at it.

What you consume ends up consuming you. What started off as some light entertainment or a guilty pleasure to has led to something more. Now you're bought into the storyline and the characters of that new Netflix series. You're sharing your opinions with others who watch it. You're in too deep. Now they know you as someone who watches that show, it's the first thing they ask about when they see you. It replaces other conversations. It's part of your identity and has started to define you. All you wanted was a bit of harmless TV.

The only way you can Netflix your way to success is if you own Netflix. Consumption is more than just box sets. It's stopping you fulfilling your potential. Silicon Valley professionals with Harvard MBAs are working continuously on creating apps and websites that deliberately get us hooked. You're scrolling social media feeds, consuming everything everyone is posting. Now you know everything about their lives, to what end? You feel worse about your own because you're comparing yourself. You want that trip, that life, that body. Your thoughts and conversations become about what others are doing and experiencing. You're less focused on your own game because you're watching others play theirs.

It's in your power to control what you consume and what you ignore. No one is forcing you to scroll, you could make other plans. You could produce. Produce good vibes, produce positivity, produce books, articles, videos, anything that gives to the world and others. As Neil Gaiman said, "Make good art". Keep making it. Keep producing your art and putting it out there and have others consume it for the good of their lives and yours. Draw up the plans and make them happen.

Writer Brianna Wiest, who has published thousands of articles, asserts, "Everybody has ideas for books and songs and companies and businesses. They remain ideas unless they are married to purpose and productivity." Author and entrepreneur Daniel Priestley said, "The book that changes your life isn't one you read, it's the one you write." Find your purpose and get producing.

What you consume can consume you. What you produce can feed you forever. Years later, someone could be inspired by something you put out there in the world. Your art can transcend language, time and distance barriers. It will exist long after you are gone. Years later you won't even remember who won that reality TV show.

Look at your producing versus consuming balance and tip the scales in favour of creating, producing and publishing over scrolling, checking and clicking. Produce more than you consume.

"If you would not be forgotten as soon as you are dead and rotten, either write things worth reading or do things worth writing."

Ben Franklin

Should You Start A Side Project?

Please don't go head first into a side project. Don't let the word "side" trick you. Whatever it is, it will take up a significant time of your time and energy. It will be part of your story. It could make or break you. Give the decision the consideration it deserves.

My definition of a side project is another venture of any kind, which is in some way separate to your main line of work. This could be the decision to start a new business, begin an MBA, sit on a board or committee, become a non-exec director, write a novel or even begin investing. It's anything that changes how you spend your time or adds another line to your bio.

For every side project that has gone amazingly well there are countless others that caused nothing but a distraction. Here are the questions to consider when deciding if you should start a side project.

What if you put all that energy into your main role?

Before considering the endless possibilities of side projects, think about what you could achieve if all your energy and enthusiasm were channelled into your current role, to grow your business or progress in your job. What if all you need is some motivation to do that? What if this compelling urge to start a side project is just a compelling urge to learn more, progress or enjoy your work better? Could this go 100% into your main venture?

Businessman Warren Buffet is a big fan of focus, citing it as the single biggest reason for his success. He said, "Really successful people say no to almost everything", they keep things simple, kill busy work and focus on fewer, higher quality bets. Jason Fried, founder of Basecamp, proudly describes himself as a non-serial entrepreneur. He put all his eggs in one basket and that basket now has over 2 million customers. Could you do less, but do it better?

Make a plan for what your main venture could look like if it had your undivided attention. The best view often comes after the hardest climb! You might be redirecting your attention prematurely. What about if you invested more, either time or cash? Put your all into it and see if you can take it from a plateau to a new level that makes you excited to work there. If, after doing this, you're still not happy, perhaps it's time to hand over, leave or sell your main project. You could follow the guidance of Tim Ferriss in 4-Hour Work Week and delegate, automate or eliminate processes to ensure your daily involvement is reduced, or you could find a buyer.

Why do you need a side project?

Perhaps your main venture is a job that you don't see as a career job; perhaps it's just there to pay the bills. Emma Jones, founder of small business network Enterprise

Nation and author of Working 5-9: How To Start A Successful Business In Your Spare Time is an advocate of working on a side project between the hours of 5 and 9pm, after you're home from your main role. That way, you give it time and energy without taking any risks. The goal of this 5-9 is that one day it could overtake the 9-5 and become the main focus.

Are you considering a side project because you're bored of your main venture? Perhaps you're feeling demotivated or have stopped learning. Perhaps you feel like you're coasting and you're looking for a new challenge. Here's where you shouldn't underestimate how much energy it takes to coast! You might be putting more than you realise into just keeping matters stable. A side project could completely unsettle that.

If you're in this lull, you have three options. One is "do nothing", where you continue to coast without beginning a new project. Who knows, you might even start to enjoy this! Take life slower, live within your means and just chill out. Not convinced? The second option is to fall back in love with your main venture. The third is to begin a side project, which could take place straight away or after you've sufficiently tested and discounted coasting or growing as viable alternatives.

What gives?

When making any decision that affects how you spend your time, think of a pie chart. Picture how your time is split across your day at the moment and then work out where this new side project fits in.

Eric Ries, author of the Lean Startup, advocates the lean startup methodology, which enables you to test the viability of a project or idea, and the existence of a customer base, before fully committing. However, undertaking even just this exercise for a side project is an outlay of time and energy away from something else.

The effort you give your side project; setting it up, running it, thinking about it, and marketing it, all has to come from somewhere. Will you be forgoing your downtime? Time spent with family and friends? Will it come from the time currently spent on your main venture? If so, what's the likely impact of that? Nothing happens in a vacuum. What are you prepared to give up, especially if you're already too busy? Time and attention are your only finite resources. Underestimate this at your peril!

Does it add or multiply?

In a recent conversation about side projects with Daniel Priestley, entrepreneur and author of several business books including Key Person of Influence, Daniel introduced the question, "Does it add or multiply?" If a side project *adds*, it adds work, adds learning, research and energy requirements that do not contribute or benefit your other ventures in any way. If a side project *multiplies*, it can serve to improve or increase the value gleaned from existing projects.

In Priestley's case, his Key Person of Influence book has associated courses and events with the same title. Within the book, he outlines why entrepreneurs should write their own book, so it makes perfect sense that another business of his is a book publishing company! If side projects *add* then you create distractions, hindrance and misdirected energy. If side projects *multiply*, you create an empire.

Rand Fishkin, founder of SaaS tool Moz and author of Lost and Founder, began Moz as a search-engine optimisation (SEO) blog, designed to share expertise, whilst running an agency in the same field. Moz (or SEOmoz, as it was formerly known) started as a forum for SEO professionals, but soon ended up overtaking the agency's turnover. It was a natural progression for Rand to turn his full attention to his side project.

Be careful moving more than one iteration away from your current knowledge base. In the book Outliers, by Malcolm Gladwell, he repeatedly refers to the "10,000-Hour Rule", relating to the hours required to become an expert in a field. Although the authors of the original study have since disputed Gladwell's usage of the concept, it holds true that a certain time outlay is required in order to reach a level of proficiency in any field. 10,000 hours is equal to 6 hours per day, of perfect and deliberate practice, for 4.5 years. No matter how fast you can learn or pick up a new skill, there's little to be gained in starting at the bottom.

Is it part of a strategy?

The organisation Free Code Camp, which helps people learn to code for free, regularly discusses side projects and why they are so important. Google employees are encouraged to spend 20% of their time on side projects. But the world of tech is a different beast. Developers are encouraged to play and experiment, which often means creating new tools. A side project can be dreamt up, created and shipped very quickly, then become a success on its own after picking up initial traction. Even if it doesn't, the experimenting and playing has benefits to the developer's main project.

This all forms part of a strategy to create talented and resourceful coders, and is an example of multiplying, not adding. It's very different to learning and setting up a whole new, separate venture that needs day-to-day running.

If you're considering a side project, don't just ensure it fits with your overall strategy; plan the best-case scenario and the worse case scenario. It's easy to daydream about the best-case scenario, but if it all goes wrong, what will you have gained?

Do you just want to scratch an itch?

If you've worked on something for a while, achieved a certain level of success than reached a plateau, it's common to begin looking around for new challenges to undertake. If this is the case, why not do your side project for fun rather than as a business venture?

Once someone pays you for a product or service, you're the supplier and they're the client. You have obligations. What if that takes the joy out of it? What if, instead, you saw your side project as a hobby? Love baking cakes and want to start selling them? Just make them for free, whenever you like! Don't charge for anything related to your side project. Look for the least-committal way of scratching that itch. You can then pick it up and drop it whenever you feel like it, before you buy that domain name!

Starting a side project might be the right decision for you, but the cost of getting it wrong is higher than you think. Take each question above into consideration before taking the leap.

"Some cause happiness wherever they go; others whenever they go."

Oscar Wilde

One Bad Egg

You have put your heart and soul into building up your business from scratch to get it to where it is today. Countless late nights, countless early mornings, to build something that you are proud of, that makes a real, positive difference to the lives of your clients and your team.

No one knows the hours you have put in. No one knows how much effort you have put into developing yourself and those around you, not to mention sales, admin and hiring. Your business scales and you have to let go of some of the things that you once looked after.

You train and you trust. Train others how to do it, trust them to deliver. Sometimes it goes well, sometimes it doesn't. Sometimes your training isn't good enough. Sometimes they're not good enough.

Never feel you have to apologise for holding someone else to the high standards you hold yourself to. Ask 'why' more. Why am I micromanaging you? Because I don't trust that you can do this. Why am I pulling you up on your actions? Because they're not good enough. Why aren't you getting the progression you want? Because you don't warrant it.

When growing a business you cannot underestimate the toxic environment that can be created from one bad egg. What starts as gossip and whispers turns to an eye roll across the room, then private messages, then to downright vicious and malicious lies. The good eggs will stay out of it. Those on the fence will join in. The ringleader will play the victim. You will find yourself genuinely wondering if they are deliberately sabotaging everything or if they are just plain stupid. Either way, it doesn't matter, you have to get them out as soon as possible. Out of your business, out of your head, out of the minds of those they have intoxicated.

The bad egg is toxic, make no mistake. They will speak as if they are the spokesperson of "everyone", but won't be able to specify who "everyone" refers to. They will speak as if they are the victim, powerless to change anything, even if they were in a position where they could. They won't be happy unless there is an "us" and "them" situation. They will dramatise every situation. They will talk behind your back, they will find a common enemy, they will roll their eyes and always have a hidden meaning in their words.

Get them out, at all costs. However, you do it, however much it costs you, get them out. Breathe a sigh of relief. Focus on the awesome team you have around you. Continue to flourish together.

"Great spirits have always
encountered opposition from
mediocre minds."

Albert Einstein

"Big jobs usually go to the men who
prove their ability to outgrow the small
ones."

Ralph Waldo Emerson

The Three People Whose Advice You Should Take

At a crossroads and working out which way to turn? Got a niggling feeling you should be trying out different tactics in your life or business? Receiving and implementing advice can make or break you, depending on whom you take it from. Here are the three people whose advice you should take:

Been there and done it

The advice of someone who has been through the exact challenge you are facing is someone whose advice is worth listening to. Whether they succeeded or learned from the experience, their knowledge and insights will be those you can't get elsewhere. Business owners face common challenges whilst business owners in the same industry often face nearly identical challenges. Make the most of the advice from those who have trodden the path you're about to tread.

Chris Reynolds, founder of The Business Method, asks two questions before taking advice. The first is, "Has the person giving me advice created the results I want to create?" and the second is "If I knew what to do, what would I do?" Verifying the guidance you hear whilst backing yourself to find the right solution is a powerful combination that might lead to taking more effective action sooner.

A caveat to this advice; when did they do it? Solving certain problems in different technological or economical circumstances might not qualify someone to solve them right now. It's easy for someone to look back fondly over a time and create a narrative around what they did and why it was so effective, forgetting mistakes or hardships that came with working through it.

Apply your own filter to this advice and think it through fully to ensure it's applicable to you.

Shares your values and knows you well

One business coach I know works solely with clients running large, impressive businesses seemingly at the expense of their physical and mental health. I know that this coach had a similar lifestyle when running his own business. It's obvious that his values and his version of "normal" and "success" have been taken on board by his clients, perhaps subconsciously. You become a combination of the people you spend most time with and before long your beliefs are shaped by theirs.

Shared values are paramount because one person's heaven can be another person's hell, depending on their individual life goals. An author I know prices his books as low as possible to be read by as many people as possible, so he can secure high ticket speaking gigs all over the world, whilst living in an eight bedroom house in

London and raising three kids. Another author prices her books far higher, but turns down offers for speaking gigs and lives in a studio flat with no commitments at all whilst travelling the world on the royalties. Same job title, different values.

I don't believe that you have to share the exact same values and beliefs in order to give and receive advice effectively, but I do believe you need to optimise for the same outcomes and I find it helpful to think in this way. In strength training, optimising for a competition two weeks away or one 6 months away will require a different training programme. Business is the same. Optimising to raise investment and sell in 5 years will require different actions to optimising for a lifestyle business that enables you to keep a team size as small as is feasible.

Before you take advice, from anyone at all, communicate your goals. Even before you start to work through a solution on your own, write down what you're trying to achieve and make sure the advice takes you closer.

Your customers

Your clients' advice on how you best serve their needs is invaluable. Blue chip companies spend millions on customer experience surveys to gather as much information as they can. If a client tells you how you could do better: listen. Their advice might be in their own best interests, sure, but aren't you there to serve their best interests?

For a company creating technology products, the advice and feedback of its users often forms the road map of new features and improvements that the developers work on, which wouldn't be possible without it.

From another article, *eight ways to have better relationships with your clients*, the foundation of great client relationships is two-way communication and the ability to take suggestions on board. Listening carefully, repeating it back, then deciding what to do will mean you filter out the unreasonable requests and action those that will lead to happier clients you love to work with, who love to work with you in return.

When should you ignore advice?

According to Napoleon Hill, "The number one reason people fail is because they listen to their friends, family and neighbours." Whilst that feels extreme, Hill might have a point! In Joy, a film about a lady who founds a business dynasty despite difficult circumstances, her family is filled with naysayers. Each member she engages with has an opinion on what she should and shouldn't be doing at any given time. Each piece of advice is clouded with the judgment of their own successes and shortcomings, plus often Joy didn't actually ask for it! The film's synopsis stipulates, "Allies become adversaries and adversaries become allies." Take advice from true allies, not those who can flit in between being your friend and foe.

How much advice you ask for is key. Jane Sparrow, culture specialist and author of Bank Of Me said, "Some of us take advice too much and end up either confused or trying to please everyone. Others ask for too little and take the trial and error route to learning." An exercise Jane recommends to her clients is to "Find someone you know talks sense and ask them to give you advice, of their choice." You never know what you might hear!

Ignore advice when you are confident with your plan and you haven't asked for it. Ignore advice when you want very different things to the person offering it. Ignore short-sighted advice that isn't well thought through. Avoid advice you will feel compelled to take, or guilty if you don't take. Avoid advice from someone who hasn't experienced something at least vaguely similar.

The best and most valuable advice is from someone with relevant experience, who understands your values and your goals. They help you make decisions and solve problems by thinking through solutions, making suggestions, challenging you, then extrapolating the advice into the future to predict what will happen if you go a certain way. Moreover, they won't be offended if you don't take it. Once you find that person, don't let them go!

"It is our choices, Harry, that show what we truly are. Far more than our abilities."

Albus Dumbledore

How
To
Live
A
Miserable
Life

Take everything personally. Make everything about you. Form an opinion on whatever you see or hear. Seek out news and gossip. Never miss a "breaking news" update. Watch reality TV and talk about the contestants. Scroll your social media feeds as soon as you wake up. Set all notifications to 'on'. Maximise your screen time. Blame others for your problems. Fail to take responsibility for your career and relationships not being where you want them to be. Flit between strategies. Believe the hype. Don't look to improve. Believe you already know everything there is to know. Feel entitled to get that job or that promotion. Compare your life to others. Make excuses. Ignore feedback. Obsess over your exes. Troll people online. Be the victim. Bitch about your friends when they can't hear. Turn up late to meet them. Never apologise. Hold grudges. Rely on alcohol. Follow the crowd. Ask the universe to solve your problems. Give up easily.

Everyone has bad days, that's cool. But when one bad day turns into a bad week, a bad month and a bad year, something needs to happen to break the cycle and change your trajectory.

Find comfort in the fact that you've taken yourself to this place, so you have the power to take yourself out of it. Nothing is impossible and breaking habits can be done. Take them one by one. Work on those things completely in your control and ignore the rest. Out of our control: the passing of time and the opinions of others. In our control:

what we think, say and do. What we let affect our mood. How we conduct ourselves, what we wear, how we spend our time.

You have the power to break old habits and start new ones that will take you further from misery and further toward happiness, but you need to take the first step in doing so. This isn't for anyone else to sort out; the world owes you nothing. Look yourself in the mirror, say "I've got this" loudly and confidently. Let's begin.

"Don't put in average effort and claim that you want exceptional results."

James Clear

Make Saying No Your Superpower

I used to want a really full diary with constant trips, social events and things to do. I wanted to be busy all the time, to tire myself out each day, then hit the pillow and wake up raring to go for the next one. I saw busy as a measure of success and linked my sense of achievement to how many emails I received or how much the phone rang.

So much has changed. Now, blank space in my diary is a sign of success. I travel for one month in every three instead of sporadic, smaller trips. Fewer emails is a sign that matters are being expertly taken care of by those in my team. I follow the "hell yeah or no rule" introduced by Derek Sivers. If something isn't a "hell yeah", it has to be a "no". Saying no to more gives me space to breathe and relax and make sure that I can give 100% to commitments I do say yes to.

Guard the blank space

Blank space in your diary is not there to be filled with whomever wants to give you things to fill it with. If you've planned a day of nothingness, guard it fiercely against helping people move house or taking people to the airport. Your time and headspace is worth more than a removal van or taxi would cost to hire. Who knows, you could have a million dollar idea on that day, because you've cleared the room to think one up. Don't undervalue your downtime.

Make the no easy

Create a "sorry I can't" email signature, that you click and personalise each time you need to decline. Keep it polite; give thanks for the invitation, but decline with a fair reason. That reason can be anything you want – it's your time to allocate. "I'm sorry I can't I already have plans" is just as valid as "I'm sorry I can't because I'm focusing on x right now." For more clarity, and to make saying no even easier, set up a "now page" and include it in your auto responder.

Sinking dread or freeing relief

Weigh up which feeling you'd rather feel. The sense of relief at declining something you just don't want to do, or saying yes and having that sinking dread the day before when you realise what your tomorrow entails. It might be three months in the future at the moment, but some day it will be tomorrow.

Cultivate selective ignorance

If you're on all the mailing lists, have all the notifications and alerts then you will know about everything that's going on, all the time, and you'll feel an obligation to get involved. Unsubscribe, change your home page and turn off the alerts. If it's really unmissable, someone will tell you.

Respond accordingly

There's a huge difference between a perfectly personalised and thoughtful letter and a mass email. If the approach to you has been careless, don't feel like you have to respond. Give it the thinking time it warrants. Not all invitations were created equal.

Say no: events you don't really care about, people who drain you, obligations you don't want to be held to. Say yes: opportunities that make you go wow, people you love to hang out with, places and work that fit with your purpose.

This isn't about being a social recluse and signing yourself out of seeing people and getting involved forever. This is about guarding your time and your attention so that when you get involved, you do it properly. This is about being able to tackle the projects that will make the most difference because you're not flitting about doing the things that anyone could do. Your time and your attention are your biggest assets, not to be given away lightly.

"In life, from the simplest thing to the biggest thing, I want to be proud of what it is and stake my claim: 'That's mine and that's how I do it.'"

Ken Block

The Grass Might Not Be Greener

An electrician I know is bored of electricity and has switched career to become a professional videographer. A videographer I know now only makes videos as a hobby so he can build his IT and web business. The head of a website agency I work with dreams of making it as a musician. A musician I know just wants to be a schoolteacher. An ex-schoolteacher is retraining as a psychologist. The cycle goes on.

One great thing about today's working world is that, at any given time, you can choose a different path and begin a completely new journey.

But what if that means we are in a constant state of believing the grass is always greener? What if by not sticking at a career, through tough times and all, the workforce of today misses out on the satisfaction and rewards that can be gleaned from longevity? What if the grass isn't actually greener?

It's easy to want to progress. Up a career ladder, up a pay grade or up the pecking order. It's easy to want what someone else has, or be persuaded by a recruiter. It's harder to not take your current reality for granted. Sometimes it's hard to remember just how good you have it at this very second.

If it's so easy to change tack at any given opportunity, where's the incentive to stay, to focus, and to build something really great?

What happens when you shift your attention, find a new career or start a new business, and then realise that you just switched problems a, b and c for problems x, y and z? You still need to solve the problems, but now you need to learn the solution from scratch. Daily challenges you once had the exact answer to are now taking over your day and you're at the bottom of a steep learning curve because you put yourself there.

I've seen people make disastrous career moves based on a case of grass is always greener. They took for granted how good they had it, they were blinded by some bright lights – then guess what? Same sh*t, different company. Except now you're further back than you were before, peddling furiously to keep up, just to prove to anyone that will listen that you made the right decision. The honeymoon period fades. It always does. Then it's onto the next fix, like a drug addict stuck answering their short-term impulses.

Flit about like this forever – always give up when it's hard – and you'll be lapped again and again by those who didn't give in. Leave your job when you're really good at it. Until then, just be exceptional and think long term.

I'm not saying that you should force yourself to do work you don't enjoy. I'm not saying it's not ok to change your mind. I'm saying be realistic about what you're entering into and don't be fooled into thinking that there won't be challenges to overcome with any new path you take. Be honest with yourself. Do you need to find different, less challenging problems or do you need to get better at dealing with those you have? Everyone, in any profession, has parts of it that they would rather not have. Soon the honeymoon phase you enter will become your new normal and you risk having jumped ship without going anywhere.

Here's how I see it, for my own life and career: Everything that I am doing right now, I will be doing forever. I will never underestimate the benefits gleaned from continuing to relentlessly put the work in when others around me are becoming distracted and veering off course. It's a strategy of consistency, longevity, incremental gains and futureproofing. Some years there will be small growth, some huge, some we'll stay the same and regroup. I'm no more or less likely to change my plan in any of those phases.

Operating in this way means I can handle blips in the road because I know the general trend is up. I'm not sidetracked from anything I see on Instagram. I can support my friend opening her own coffee shop without feeling like I want one too. It means I can take inspiration from success stories without envy of any kind.

If you know your own mind and your own path, you will never be hit with a case of grass is always greener. Each move you make will be thought-through and on purpose.

You'll have the wisdom and the foresight to differentiate between genuine opportunities and distractions in disguise.

"Who then is invincible? The one who cannot be upset by anything outside their reasoned choice."

Epictetus

Is Work-life Balance Overrated?

Two-thirds of entrepreneurs sacrifice their personal wellbeing in the pursuit of success. Research carried out by Investec Private Bank found that entrepreneurs regard having a happy and healthy workforce as a key success signal, but that they do not prioritise their own happiness in the same way.

In the study, 68% of entrepreneurs said the importance of a work-life balance is exaggerated; meaning that they accept their work may invade their personal life. In fact, 64% said a poor work-life balance is a "necessary sacrifice" to achieve success and 61% said they "never stop thinking about work". But why is this the case and do businesses really benefit from their owners working overtime?

Employee wellbeing is topical right now. The best employers are putting research and energy into how to create a workplace where people want to be, which enables them to deliver their best work. The Sunday Times' annual list of the best places to work rewards businesses that place importance on the wellbeing of their team. The study found that for 39% of entrepreneurs, included in their definition of success is, "Creating a business where people are happy".

Business owners see a direct correlation between the happiness and health of their team members in doing great work and their business progressing, but fail to include their own happiness and wellbeing when evaluating the success of their business. In fact, they likely see an inverse relationship, in that their own success has to come at a cost of their own health and wellbeing.

This could be because they think they are exempt from needing intervention, or perhaps they don't feel that they need the separation in the same way.

In either case, when entrepreneurs are talking about the wellbeing of their team they are not including themselves. They are not including themselves in their team wellbeing programmes and, by definition; they are prizing their employee's wellbeing over their own. The study also found that 42% of business owner respondents regularly have fewer than six hours of sleep each night.

When starting out in business, it's likely that a business-owner's focus is purely on their work; setting up, product design and development, meeting prospects, marketing, delivery and finances. It might be only when this set up phase is complete that the idea of work-life balance is even considered, possibly in response to experiencing burnout or receiving comments from concerned friends and family members. In many cases it's only when hiring team members that employee wellbeing comes into play at all. Now there are mouths to feed and other people's needs to consider.

They know there is no risk of them leaving their own business, therefore they can make unreasonable demands of themself and they can expect work all around the clock. However, they also know they cannot expect this of the people around them; therefore they are forced to operate a different approach to care.

In the TV show Mad Men, about the advertising agencies of Madison Avenue in the 1960s, the account executives regularly pull all-nighters to deliver for demanding clients. But times have changed since then. At my social media agency, I fiercely protect the boundaries of my team members. I wouldn't expect responses to emails on evenings and weekends. I don't call someone out-of-hours and I want the people I employ to make the absolute most of their non-work time. I want someone to clock off at 5pm and not feel like they have to stay all evening. I want someone to give 100% to their life when at home so they can give 100% to their work when at work. Do I guard my own boundaries this much? Probably not.

I don't think I'm alone in this. So why don't business owners practise what they preach? Do business owners have an optimistic sense of what they can handle, or are they just more resilient?

Perhaps when it's your own business you don't feel the need to split work and life so definitely. But what if business owners are suckers for punishment and believe that the price for the independence and success must be paid in hours and old-fashioned slog? If someone has a happy team and a successful business, does it matter how they're feeling in their own mind? Of course it does!

In the 4-Hour Work Week, Tim Ferriss' book on lifestyle design, he challenges business owners to regularly ask themselves the question "Am I being productive or am I inventing things to do to avoid the important?" There's a big difference between essential work that moves the needle and busy work that has no real benefit. Ferriss applies Parkinson's Law and Pareto's Law here. If you allow yourself to work 80 hours per week, you'll fill that time. If you allow yourself to work only 20 hours per week, you'll make ruthless decisions and be forced to prioritise only the essential.

In It Doesn't Have To Be Crazy At Work, by Basecamp founders Jason Fried and David Heinemeier Hansson, they shared stories of Basecamp's ethos to employee (and founder) wellbeing. It involves having scheduled time for deep work with no interruption, no meetings whatsoever and simply refusing to entertain the unhealthy work culture of other tech companies in their industry. The authors put forward that they have succeeded *because* of this way of working, not *despite* it.

On the flipside, is constantly thinking about work necessarily a bad thing? What if a business owner loves their work, their clients and their team? What if constantly thinking of ideas on how they can improve and deliver more value is their favourite thing to do? Are those people obsessed with others finding 'balance' just resentful that they haven't found their own true calling? Just like different people require different levels of sleep and food, what if "balance" is subjective, too?

"All work and no play makes Jack a dull boy", as The Shining proclaims. Maybe, but what if Jack's work involves curing disease, saving lives and driving cutting-edge innovation? What if Jack just loves his work? Is that dull?

I believe that if an entrepreneur can run a flourishing and happy business as well as staying active, having varied interests, maintaining close friendships, running a home and getting enough sleep, they are winning at life. I also believe it's not that easy. However, I have found that putting my own wellbeing as the number one priority has exponential benefits to my team, my clients and my business.

In aeroplane safety messages, cabin crew advise that you "fit your own oxygen mask before helping others". James Altucher dedicates a whole book to imploring readers to "Choose Yourself". Arianna Huffington's book Thrive looks into the heightened sense of purpose and focus someone accesses after a good night's sleep. It's sound advice from people who have been there before.

As a business owner, you are one of your company's most prized assets. The role of a successful leader, founder or CEO involves being laser-focused on strategy, delegating effectively and not missing anything. It's a sharpness that can only be accessed from a healthy mind and body and anyone that says otherwise is fooling themselves or making excuses.

Great things will happen when a business owner's downtime, me-time and gym-time is seen less as an opportunity cost and more as an investment. It's not about how much low quality work you can get done over the entirety of the week; it's about making the most of the hours you put in.

"Be tolerant with others and strict with yourself."

Marcus Aurelius

10 Ways To Stop Your Smartphone Ruining Your Life

Let's never take the power of technology for granted. It can unite communities, enable completely new ways of working and level the playing field for millions. However, it's well documented that internet and device usage comes with diminishing returns. We win at life when we are in control of the devices and props that we use to facilitate our day-to-day. We lose at life when they control us.

In Cal Newport's book, Digital Minimalism, he differentiates between compulsory and optional technologies. Compulsory technologies are those devices, apps and actions that you absolutely need to do, to keep your job and pay your bills. Optional technologies include everything else. Within the book he advises that readers conduct an analysis on those technologies that are compulsory and optional to them, then take steps to reduce or eliminate those they deem optional.

In Thrive, by Arianna Huffington, she talks about training your mind to resist checking your smartphone. It's not easy, but it can be done and she describes the benefits in happiness and wellbeing of achieving this level of control over your device.

Addiction is defined as a compulsion towards a particular substance or activity. The Center for Internet and Technology Addiction has designed a test that you can take to see if you're addicted to your phone. Being addicted to something, including your smartphone, specific apps or the internet in general zaps your energy, reduces productivity and has harmful implications including anxiety, compulsion and inability to focus.

In a nutshell, the way you stop your smartphone ruining your life is by using it less. Sounds simple, but unless there's a plan in place it probably won't happen. Here's the plan:

1. Wear a watch

If every time you want to check the time you reach for your phone, you run the risk of regularly starting the spiral of scrolling and checking that you're trying to avoid. In James Altucher's book, Choose Yourself, he talks about the *loop* he finds himself in whenever he picks up a device. Checking his blog comments, Twitter mentions, Amazon rankings and others is a 20-minute loop that he can do multiple times per day if he's not careful.

Part of not letting your smartphone ruin your life is breaking habits. Wear a watch and reduce the number of times you need to pick it up all together.

2. Buy an alarm clock

Start your day the best possible way by being in control of it. If your smartphone is your alarm clock, it's the first thing you touch in the morning, which probably means your first few minutes are dictated by whatever happens to be on your screen. If that's a new text or an email you need to respond to, suddenly you're not in control of how you spend your time. Buy an alarm clock that goes next to your bed and wakes you up without you needing to touch your phone, and then only pick your device up once you're washed, dressed and ready to attack the day.

3. Get better at describing and remembering

You're in a conversation and trying to name that actor in that film that was also in that other film. Or you're talking about that video you saw of that dog doing that cool thing with the frisbee at the Superbowl The next thing you know, you're pulling out your phone to look it up or to show your mate. Instead of giving in to this compulsion, cultivate your skills in remembering and describing. If you can always Google something, your brain learns that it doesn't need to retain information. It learns to rely on your smartphone. Furthermore, if you can always show someone a picture, you won't need to be good at describing anything. Practice recalling information and picture telling stories without the need for visual aids. It's an art.

4. Set some rules

It seems crazy that our smartphones can connect with long lost friends from all over the world, yet we use them just as often to ignore the close friends right in front of us. There's a word, "phubbing", that means snubbing someone by being on your phone in their company. The person opposite you wants to spend time with you, as you do with them. You're not going to live forever, your time on this planet is finite and then you'll never see them again, so make the most of them whilst they're here and give them your attention. This includes your kids, your parents and your friends. Some personal rules I follow: don't use your phone in company; don't use your phone when you're walking somewhere. The first is to develop friendships; the second is to avoid walking into lampposts.

5. Use the screen time monitor

Apple iPhones have a feature whereby they monitor your screen time and give you usage reports, including percentage change week to week. In 2017 the average American adult spent 2 hours and 51 minutes on their phone each day. Paying attention to this information is useful for gaining awareness of how much you're looking at a screen. However, don't just swap one screen for another. It's all very well deleting Facebook from your phone but if you're just going to use it on your laptop you haven't changed your actions, just swapped which screen you're looking at. Read a book, get outside, go for a meal – find alternatives to looking at screens all together.

6. Use the downtime function

Another feature of the iPhone is the ability to set a downtime timer, where your apps are blocked and out of use unless you manually override the block. My smartphone is set to 'downtime' between 9:30pm and 7:30am. One day soon it will be 8:30pm and 8:30am but I'm taking baby steps! See what you can do and experience how good it feels.

7. Turn off notifications

I read an article from the blog of Joel Gascoigne, founder of Buffer, whereby he conducted an experiment and turned all his smartphone notifications off. Notifications, really, are someone else's priorities entering your space. Joel discovered that, at first, turning notifications off led to him checking apps more regularly, but then he grew to enjoy not having any, even saying, "I came to love the fact that nothing came onto my lock screen or lit up my phone." and notes its positive influence on his focus and productivity, "with zero notifications, I feel like I can get my head stuck into a problem much more easily than I did before. I never realised when I had those notifications on that they truly could throw me off my current thought and cause me difficulty getting that focus back." Join the zero notification movement and see if it works for you!

8. Batch activities

It's your choice. You could check your emails, messenger and social networks every five minutes, or you could check them once a day and whizz through deleting, responding and delegating in one go. I'd wager that doing that latter would take far less time and break your concentration far less. What else could you batch? In Greg McKeown's Essentialism, his motto is "Less, but better". Less checking email regularly but better responses when you do, because you're focused on one task. Less checking social networks throughout the day but more enjoyment when you commit to catching up with your newsfeed once in the evening.

9. Switch to greyscale

If the above haven't reduced your smartphone usage, try this. On your iPhone, go to settings > general > accessibility. Then under the 'vision' setting locate "greyscale" and toggle on. This setting turns your entire phone to greyscale and makes it look far less inviting. The app icons for social media platforms are designed to be bright, colourful and inviting. They're designed to catch your attention and pull you in. Take away their power by making them look very boring indeed!

10. Have a higher purpose

Finally, and perhaps the most philosophical of all the ten ways to stop your smartphone ruining your life, is to have a higher purpose. Were you really put here, on this planet, to scroll apps, live on WhatsApp and respond to emails? Of course you weren't! If you're allowing yourself to get distracted easily, do you need to look further inside and find out what you're trying so hard to avoid?

Addiction and compulsion is one thing, but procrastination to avoid your work is another. Find a role doing work you get happily absorbed by, actively cultivate conversation with the person right in front of you, pick up a new sport or hobby, or just hang out with people who make you forget to check your phone.

"I do not try to dance better than anyone else. I only try to dance better than myself."

Mikhail Baryshnikov

Only
Do
Work
You
Would
Happily
Do
For
Free

If you had to do your job and not get paid for it, would you still do it? One step further – if you had to pay in order to do what you do, would you take the hit? University students in the UK spend nearly £10,000 per year to access the learning and opportunities their degree course brings. Would you do the same for your career?

I've met people who only do their job for the money and they're usually boring as hell. They just don't care about their work, clients, colleagues, anything. They don't speak about their profession or industry with any passion or enthusiasm and it feels more like a burden to them than a choice. The week is a slog and the weekend is an escape. Work is work and life is life – they're completely different people in each scenario and they aggressively protect the line between them.

It doesn't matter what they're selling as long as someone is buying it. It doesn't matter how much they dread Monday morning as long as the compensation is attractive. Put this person in a managerial position and it fails spectacularly. They assume everyone else is only there for the cash and become fixated on salary, failing to ignite or develop anyone else's passion in their role.

Based on the fact that you're not going to live forever, I believe that the business you start or the job you commit to should be something you would do for free. Or even, something you'd happily lose money doing.

"Your work is going to fill a large part of your life, and the only way to be truly satisfied is to do what you believe is great work. And the only way to do great work is to love what you do."

- Steve Jobs

I was recently interviewed for the Connectt podcast and asked why I started a social media agency. My response was that I didn't set out to start a business; I set out to do the work I enjoyed to do. All I wanted to do was spend every day writing fun and creative social media posts for different companies. The fact that it became an agency of 18 social media managers was a result of expanding that passion and finding other great people to work with who shared it.

Best-selling horror writer Stephen King said "I've made a great deal of dough from my fiction, but I never set a single word down on paper with the thought of being paid for it... I have written because it fulfilled me. Maybe it paid off the mortgage on the house and got the kids through college, but those things were on the side – I did it for the buzz. I did it for the pure joy of the thing. And if you can do it for the joy, you can do it forever."

Are you doing it for the joy or the money? What if the money wasn't there, would you still do it?

"The secret of joy in work is contained in one word –
excellence. To know how to do something well is to enjoy
it."

- Pearl S. Buck

In Gary Vaynerchuk's 2008 TED talk, Do What You Love
(No Excuses) he urges the audience to "Stop doing stuff
you hate!" because "you can lose just as much money
being happy as hell!" Whatever you do, don't do it just for
the money. Do it for the purpose, the vision, the thrills
and the fun. Do it for the flow you find when you're deep
in your work. Do it for the stories or because there's an
itch that you just have to scratch. Do it because you really
believe you're onto something. Do it for where it might
lead, just don't do it for the money.

I once went to an event where Rob Hallmark, founder of
men's fragrance Gruhme, was speaking. He asked the
audience of entrepreneurs "If you were given £500,000,
right now, would you spend it on the business you're
currently running?" I was astounded at how many people
said no. If you'd take an easy escape at any given
moment, you're in the wrong game and you're not making
the best of your talent or your life.

There's power and strength in doing work that you
genuinely love to do. There's freedom and happiness in
truly believing that your career path is a choice that you
have made, completely of your own accord. You commit

to it because you know it's what you were put here to do. You might face challenges and setbacks, because that's what happens, but nothing can deter you or stop you from carrying on because it's all insignificant compared to what you're trying to achieve.

If you're already there, great, keep going. If not, work it out and make a plan.

"Remember, when we forfeit our right to choose, someone else will choose for us."

Greg McKeown

Decide
What To Do
With
Your Life,
Or
Someone Else
Will
Decide
For You

If you don't choose exactly how you want to spend your own time, you will forever be at the mercy of others and their ambitions for you. If you don't live your life by design, you will live your life by default. You'll flit around doing whatever feels right at the time but not really going anywhere. You'll change your mind and your vision based on whomever you spoke to last.

Make your own plan and stick to it. Decide how you're going to get to where you want to get to and be the person you want to be. Plan every single detail, and every day take steps in the right direction. String the good days together and ignore the odd bad one. Don't waste a second. Maybe it won't go exactly as planned, but that's why you need to dream bigger.

No one else will decide this for you. Any advice you take will be based on someone else's own preconceptions about what you can achieve. Don't let their limits become yours. Be honest with yourself.

You don't need anyone else's version of success clouding your own judgment. You don't need anyone else's approval to be who you want to be. Wear whatever the hell you want to wear and live wherever you want to live. Just having the courage to should be all the proof you need that it's right for you. People will look, stare, comment and pass judgment, but you won't be concerned with that because you're so sure of your path.

No one can rock your footing and no one can deter your focus.

Act out of purpose and be deliberate. Never act out of guilt or obligation. If you don't want to do something, say no. If you don't want to see someone, say no. Create free space in your diary and fill it only with those things that you'd give anything to do and those people you'd do anything to see. Every second spent on anything else means passing up those moments.

Be open to learning and taking on board new viewpoints, and don't put yourself in any boxes. Introvert or extrovert? Ambivert. Tall or short? Just right. You're not clumsy, you're not shy, you're not anything someone else has defined you as because they don't know you like you know yourself.

Please do not fool yourself into thinking that the right answer will just come to you, or the right opportunities will just find you. They won't. Find them yourself. The universe is indifferent to your needs and unconcerned with your goals. You wouldn't want it any other way because you don't need approval from anywhere else. You got this.

"I hope you aren't so wrapped up in nonessential stuff that you forget to really enjoy yourself - because this moment is about to be over. I hope you'll look back and remember today as the day you decided to make every one count, to relish each hour as if there would never be another. And when you get the choice to sit it out or dance, I hope you dance."

Oprah Winfrey

The Four Distraction Traps Business Owners Need To Avoid

My favourite Latin word is 'euthymia'. The word, as defined in Seneca's essays means:

"Believing in yourself and trusting you are on the right path, and not being in doubt by following the myriad footpaths of those wandering in every direction."

I believe that if you don't define exactly who you are and what you want to achieve, you will become so side-tracked that you end up pursuing other people's interests, short term goals, or you will carry out actions that don't progress your journey.

Here are four ways you can be side-tracked along with the ways to avoid it happening to you.

Insta-envy.

If you follow 400 people on Instagram, and once per year every one of your followers posts about something really cool they have done, you will go through the year seeing a daily occurrence of someone else doing something cool. An award someone won, a country they visited, recognition they earned, a spectacular view they saw. You might be fooled, therefore, into thinking that cool things happen to other people all the time. You might go one step further and compare all the things that you see on Instagram to your own life, and you might decide that it's not as good in comparison.

It's easy to see the daily lives of others and start to believe that they have things we want for ourselves. Instagram envy is a real thing. But actually, there are trade-offs made all the time and it's important not to forget that. Don't compare your behind-the-scenes with someone else's edited showreel. It won't lead anywhere good.

If your own vision of who you and where you want to be is absolutely crystal clear, nothing you see on Instagram can make you question it. You can follow a friend's travels around the world with interest, but zero envy. You can genuinely be happy for them and the path that they have chosen to be on, without feeling like you want parts of it for yourself.

Trying to sell to everyone.

Not only do you need to be crystal clear on your vision and how you're going to get there, you need to be crystal clear on who your audience is. If not, you will end up selling to everyone. I once met someone who hand-created beautiful shoes. When I asked who his target audience was, he said: "anyone with feet".

In your business, your target audience might be women aged 25-30. Then you meet someone selling products to 35-40 year olds and you think how you can adapt your offering to capture that market too. Before you know it, your original audience isn't as keen and your second audience doesn't believe your products were designed for them.

The children's storybooks I co-wrote are for 6-9 year-old English-speaking kids. Yes, we could do a picture book for younger kids. Yes, we could write novellas for older kids, but first we are focusing on 6-9 year olds only, and our entire brand is aimed there.

Accept that not everyone is in your target audience and that's fine. Sometimes you will need to turn potential customers down so that you can best look after your current ones. Freelance marketing consultant Tami Brehse wrote an article to explain when exactly you should turn down work. One of those times is "when the work doesn't fit your niche". She's right.

It might feel difficult to turn down potential work or potential new income streams, but the cost of taking on every piece of work you are offered is just too high. Being able to say "sorry, I can't help you with this" is a strong play. You're not someone who flits around following opportunity – you know your plan and you're sticking to it.

Taking too much advice

It's easy to be side-tracked by taking too much advice. Someone asks about your business and you tell them. They give you their idea of how your management structure should work. They talk about a revolutionary incentive scheme you should try. They tell you what worked for their business. It is incredibly easy for other people to give business or life advice, even if they know very little about you, your business and even your sector.

If you're not crystal clear on your purpose and confident of how you execute it, you are at risk of taking other people's opinions and advice on board, even if it is not right. Being advised by multiple sources means you could end up straddling strategies, confusing your customers and your team.

Solution: take the advice from the people whose life you want. Take the advice of those who have actual experience of what they are saying. Take advice from the actions of people and not just their words.

"We could do this".

You meet someone whose business has "synergy" with yours and now they want to create something that both of your audiences will be interested in. I'm not knocking joint ventures, but do them after you've made it and not before. Sure, you could do x, y and z. But if you do all three then you'll have a mediocre x, y and z when you could have a fantastic x. One at a time is the way. You don't have to do everything right now. Stay laser-focused on the one thing that will make the biggest difference.

Software as a service (SAAS) companies often have document called a product roadmap. When one of their users says, "You could add this new feature", they add it onto the product roadmap. Each potential fix or feature then follows a feasibility study to work out the exact route of the product roadmap along with timescales. Some potential features are ignored entirely. When an idea pops into your head of something you *could* do, write it down, and then focus on what you need to now. If the "could do" idea is really that amazing you won't be able to stop thinking about it. If you forget about it quickly then maybe you shouldn't consider it in the first place.

Create and define *your* vision for *your* business, *your* life and *your* success. Have confidence in your ability to follow the path to that goal and enjoy the journey it takes you on. Use other people's success as inspiration. Take the right advice and ideas on board. But, at all costs, don't be distracted.

"We are kept from our goal, not by obstacles but by a clear path to a lesser goal."

Robert Brault

Visualisation Is Not A Substitute For Hard Work

It's fine to get up each day, write in your journal, look at your vision board, say your affirmations, recite some mantras, overcome your limiting beliefs and ask the universe for everything you want. It's not fine to then sit there and scroll Facebook and wonder why it's not happening. Why is the money tree not bearing fruits? Because fruits take labour.

If you are asking the universe but turning up late to meetings, you won't get where you want to get. If you are dying to create passive income but can't convert new clients for your startup, something is going wrong. If you're chilling out in the sun but haven't got any bookings, you're not self-employed, you're unemployed. Try swapping the affirmations for networking. Try swapping the visualisation for making calls. Use those mindset exercises as a supplement to your considered actions, not a replacement.

In world champion marathon runner Paula Radcliffe's book, How to Run, she explains how she conditions her mind to win a race. One of the mental exercises Radcliffe follows is to visualise the finish line, to imagine her friends and family are there supporting her and picture the looks on their faces as they watch her win. She pictures the race time she wants to achieve on the clock displayed above her. She thinks about this before a race and throughout too, if she needs extra motivation.

Alongside the visualisation in Radcliffe's book are detailed training and diet plans, along with guidance on how to schedule your mileage before running your first marathon. Paula Radcliffe could, perhaps, have won all those races without the visualisation. But there's no way she could have won them without the training. The two complimented each other to make her the fastest female marathoner of all time. One of the main criticisms of the book is that to follow her marathon training programmes, you'd have to be a full-time runner. Of course, Radcliffe was a full time runner, reportedly running over 145 miles per week!

It's undeniable that visualisation can be a powerful tool. In an experiment conducted to demonstrate the effectiveness of visualisation in how basketball players converted free throws, the psychologist split 120 of them into four separate groups. The first group practised. The second group visualised themselves making free throws, but didn't practice. The third group undertook a combination of physical and mental practice, and the fourth group didn't do anything. The result? Groups 1 and 3 improved, group 3 by a greater proportion. Group 2 made no significant improvement.

In this example, and plenty more from the world of business, the practice itself was the foundation and the mental exercises were the edge. Visualisation by itself didn't work. In the real world, it should never be seen as a quick shortcut for missing practice or just putting the miles in.

Visualisation should help with two things: motivation and attitude. Getting good, mastering your craft and executing your plan, that's something else.

This year I have interviewed fifteen entrepreneurs, business leaders and creatives about the childhood influences that shaped their future success. The thread that ran, without fail, through each of their stories is the impact of solid, hard work. Many of them watched their parents getting up early, putting the hours in, striving to achieve success, and they emulated this to develop their own work ethic.

Among these fifteen, Craig Donaldson, the CEO of Metrobank, grew up in a pub and watched his parents share kitchen and front of house duties for 15 hours a day. He learned very early on that if customers weren't happy with the food, drink or service, they simply wouldn't return. This kind of attitude towards work meant that Donaldson, like many other successful entrepreneurs and business people, are unashamed of just working hard.

Surround yourself with positive people, yes. Set your goals and visualise achieving them, yes. Have mantras you say to yourself when you need encouragement, of course. But no amount of affirmations will substitute working out a plan and giving it everything you've got.

Remember, a plane doesn't take off because it has mentally revved itself up so it feels ready to perform. It doesn't lie dormant until it has motivated itself to start the engine. It takes off and reaches its destination because it's designed to do so. All the parts are present and working: the engine, the wings, the pilot and crew. Planes take off because of design, not desire.

There is no magic potion. There is no money tree. Nothing happens suddenly. The way to really succeed? Get 90% of your motivation purely from the fact that you're doing something you believe in, even when it's tough. Put your heart and soul into it. Keep learning, stay enthusiastic, do the right thing. Keep going.

You can't have the highs without the lows, and you absolutely cannot have the money, the freedom, the lifestyle, the accolades, the network and the opportunities without the hours of effort, sacrifice, perseverance and faith in the years leading up to that point. If anyone tries to sell you shortcuts, be very sceptical. If something sounds too good to be true, it probably is. If someone is selling a course promising that you can be a millionaire, consider that they'll sell more courses if they make it sound easy. It's not easy. Don't be fooled. Define where "there" is. If you're not there yet, keep working.

Visualisation and hard work are the perfect pairing, but the former is not a substitute for the latter.

"You can't build a reputation on what you are going to do."

Henry Ford

10 Ways To Stay Sane Whilst Running A Business

Entrepreneurs and business owners have some of the hardest jobs out there. Running a company, growing a team, managing processes and predicting the future whilst keeping quality high is a juggling act that only the best can do effectively. However, get it right and you're winning!

No matter what the world is throwing at you, here are 10 ways to stay sane whilst running a business.

1. Trust your gut

That person you weren't quite sure about? That offer that seemed too good to be true? Anything that's just a bit iffy – trust your gut feeling. Someone might be saying all the right things but if something's telling you that something isn't right, listen. Sleep on it. Say you need time to think. Process the information carefully and commit only once sure.

Laying awake at night with doubts that you've made the right decision? Get your gut involved – it knows more than you realise.

"Never ignore a gut feeling, but never believe that it's enough"

- Robert Heller

2. Say no

There's always an event you could be going to, there's always a call someone wants you to "jump on", and there are a million things asked of you at any given time. But running around the city with no time to breathe doesn't make for success or sanity. Get crystal clear on your vision, goal and plans and say no to anything that doesn't fit with that plan. Know when something is a distraction. Speculate at first, sure, but at some point you need to choose your path and stick to it, forsaking all others.

Saying no to invitations frees up calendar and space and brain space and often that's where your best work happens.

3. Take ownership

Adlerian psychology talks about a concept called *the separation of tasks* when discussing interpersonal relationships. That is; focus on your own tasks and do not interfere with the tasks of others. Nearly all business success lies in the strength of interpersonal relationships, so training others to do their tasks then trusting that they will leaves them with a clear purpose and saves you from micromanaging.

Insanity is taking everything on yourself. Ensure your team members are clear on what they need to do. Train them well then let them take ownership.

4. Grow your support network

Very few problems are unique. Others will have faced and solved the same challenges that you are facing right now. Find your support network and learn from their experience. Laugh together about how trivial it all really is.

The smaller this circle, the better, because overthinking and oversharing isn't the goal. Confide in your closest and make it look easy to everyone else.

5. Do the hard thing first

When deciding the order in which to approach your to-do list, do the hardest thing first. Solve the biggest problem head-on. Open a conversation by addressing the elephant in the room. Tackle the obstacle honestly and openly and breathe a sigh of relief when it's sorted, out of your head and frees up your attention.

What separates average business leaders from great ones is the willingness to do the hard thing because it's the right thing to do. Anyone can give good news; make big plans or fluffy promises. Not everyone can have the difficult conversations and turn around the situations everyone else thought were lost causes.

6. Competition doesn't exist

You're not competing with anyone. There's enough work to go around and this isn't a zero sum game with a winner and a loser. Stop driving yourself mad with what company X and Y are doing because it just doesn't matter.

You have more in common with people in your own industry than you think and there's no point in hostility. Besides, you just don't know what the future will bring. Stick to your own game and let everyone else stick to theirs. Focusing on so-called competitors means you underestimate yourself and overlook the strengths that make you unique.

7. Less but better

It amazes me when a business's description starts "We specialise in…" and then proceeds to reel off a lengthy list of specialisms. How can you possibly specialise in everything? I don't believe you!

Remember Gordon Ramsey's show, Kitchen Nightmares? In the 10-year series, chef Ramsey goes around restaurants and attempts to turn them around. The first thing he tackles is the menu; sometimes chopping down a multi-page dossier into a perfectly-formed set of 5-7 options. The reasoning? You simply cannot be amazing at everything. You can be mediocre at a lot of things, sure, but who wants that?

Spreading oneself too thinly can make you feel overwhelmed and out of control. Do less, but do it better.

8. Do what only you can do

If you are feeling overworked then chances are you're carrying out time-consuming tasks that don't need to be done by you. Plot your working day as a pie chart. How much of it is deep work that you and you alone can do?

Work out where your real strengths lie and train your trusted team to do everything else. Divide and conquer. Your weakness will be someone else's strength, so let them at it and watch them flourish!

"If someone else can do it, I'm not going to do it."

- Derek Sivers

9. Do the right thing

When faced with overwhelm and decisions to make, let your moral compass be the basis of your actions. Don't wish anyone harm and don't rise to the top by stepping on others. If you always do what you believe to be the right thing, you will never feel like you have anything to prove. You will sleep soundly and withstand all criticism thrown your way. Develop a reputation for being ambitious yet smart and fair and operate with the next ten years in mind, not just the next week.

10. Keep it in perspective

Worse things happen at sea. You really are fine and your problems really aren't that bad. If the general trend is up you can handle a few blips in the road. Visualise yourself rising up, above your phone and your laptop and your office and look at your company from afar. You are here, on this earth, once and once only. Find the helicopter view and act accordingly.

"Funny how some distance makes everything seem small."

Elsa, Frozen

Be Exceptional Today

The most successful people I know are laser-focused on operating at the upper limit of their ability. Always. They apply that mindset to their business, their work, their writing, their family, their hobbies, or anything they choose to focus on. They don't see the point in putting their name to anything unless they're going to give it everything.

I'm not talking about being exceptional at some point in the future. I'm not talking about looking back on your life when it's ending and congratulating yourself for doing a great job. I'm talking about being exceptional right now, this second, and being it consistently.

Carrie Green, founder of the Female Entrepreneur Association, constantly reminds her members to get intentional about their business; that success is never an accident. She advises them to succeed on purpose by visualising where they want to be and making it happen by intentionally delivering every single day. Carrie turned a blog that profiled female entrepreneurs into a multi million-dollar membership organisation by following these principles herself.

It's imperative that your commitment to being exceptional starts right now. You don't know what will happen next, but you can prepare to succeed in every eventuality. People are largely consistent, which means the mistakes and oversights of today will only serve to be exaggerated in the future. A string of bad todays doesn't make for a positive tomorrow. Rome wasn't built in a day, but they were laying bricks every hour. Doing a great job right now is the best indicator of future success.

In your business, you need to focus on being exceptional today because that's all your customers care about. They don't care about your huge growth plans, they don't care about that other huge account you won. They care about getting the service or the products you promised them, right now, to the best of your ability.

In an interview with Ben Banks, the founder of specialist sports brand SBD, he was asked what he was most likely to say at work. The answer, "Let's just double check that". Least likely to say, "That'll do". Ben's commitment to every product with the SBD name on being exceptional has meant the brand has earned a reputation of being a stickler for quality. I've heard Ben receive stick for the fact that nothing gets past his hawk eyes! But guess what? The business is thriving, SBD receives sales and global recognition from top athletes and its customers trust the quality of the products. They recommend the products to their friends and the future success of the business stakes care of itself.

Don't underestimate the power that being exceptional right now can hold in creating yourself a favourable future.

Don't underestimate the power of being known as someone who is really good at everything they put their name to. You don't need to share the hours of work and practice that went into getting there. Make it look easy. Make it your superpower.

I'm not the first person to say this and I won't be the last. You might have seen the Steve Martin quote "Be so good they can't ignore you", the wisdom of which rings true for this message.

Don't be embarrassed about having exceptionally highest standards of yourself and everyone around you. It's not a bad thing. Good sometimes isn't good enough. Something slipping in the short term doesn't bode well for the long term.

The 2009 film "He's just not that into you" brings a refreshing approach to dating and relationships. Every time a girl was stood up on a date, every time he didn't call, every time someone's other half wasn't making any effort, a line was used: "He's just not that into you". At first the characters took offence at the brutal honesty, but after considering they found it to be exactly the line they needed.

What if we took a similar approach to failing businesses? Rather than blaming market forces, ex-team members or the board, what if the answer was just, "We need to get better"? We need to be exceptional. No excuses, we're just not good enough right now. The great people around you will jump at the chance to improve too. Surround yourself with these people, rather than those who make excuses, explain it away and blame others. Be the firmly in the former camp yourself.

The recipe for becoming exceptional is a wake-up call about where you are right now coupled with the deliberate intention to succeed.

How do you get there? Put your phone away, remove the beliefs you have about what is holding you back, put yourself in the driving seat of your business and life and do the things you need to do. Be exceptional.

"[To succeed], you must study the endgame before everything else."

Grandmaster José Raúl Capablanca

How
To
Be
More
Claire
Underwood

Claire Underwood is the main character in the sixth series of House of Cards having shared the title in the first five. She's the 47th President of the United States, and the first female president, albeit fictionally. But most of all, Claire Underwood is a fascinating character. She's absolutely ruthless, she's practised and planned, she's on a mission and letting nothing stand in her way. Murder aside, we could all do with being just a little bit more Claire Underwood. Here's why:

Nothing shocks her

Urgent news just in? Breaking bulletin announced? Scandalous intelligence just received? It doesn't matter how shocking the information, Claire will absolutely not be fazed by it. She'll take the information in and she'll give nothing away; her expression will remain the same. We're so used to seeing gasps and hearing exclamations in response to news, it's a stark contrast for someone to appear nonplussed. You get the impression she already knew and you get the impression she knows exactly what to do next, giving her an all-powerful aura. Despite nothing shocking her, she'll often shock others with her big, bold moves that throw them off course and buy her time.

She thinks ten steps ahead

Claire's mind is a constant hive of "if this then that" scenarios. She's not merely talking to someone, she's pre-empting their response and she's planning how she'll respond to that. She's not operating with a best-case plan A, she's considered plans B-Z and has a counter-attack for each. She's thought of every eventuality and what each one means for her and everyone else. She knows her end game and she can see the path to it no matter the short-term nuances that are subject to change. She's not going to be sidetracked by someone else's agenda because she's just too focused.

She doesn't care what anyone thinks

People will talk. Critics will criticise. Haters gonna hate. Claire knows full well that she will be talked about and she just doesn't care. She'd much rather be talked about than not talked about; it means she's getting somewhere. Claire doesn't waste any time thinking about people who don't like her; she's working out how she can use them to her advantage. If she deems them significant, she'll win them over. If not, she'll let it slide. She knows she needs to move quickly with everything she does and worrying about the opinions of others will only slow her down.

No option is off the table

If her best friend from college lets her down, she can reveal a secret she was trusted to keep. If her husband has overstepped the mark, she can make a life without him. Claire's sees someone as her greatest ally or her worst enemy depending on their last action and she doesn't shy away from options that might be difficult or seem impossible. Considering every possibility means she is best placed to choose the most advantageous route and she sees all situations and people as disposable. She knows how to appeal to someone's own greed in order to manipulate them into doing what she wants them to. She rarely takes no for an answer.

She answers the question she wants to answer

Like a true politician, Claire hears a question and pretty much ignores it. She has her talking points, she knows the message she wants to deliver and she can take or leave the actual question asked. The result? She's operating on her own agenda at all times, she can't be caught off guard and she controls the message. You can't twist her arm; she's not going to say too much, so there's no point trying to dig. On the flipside, she carefully leaks the information she wants to get into the public domain in exactly the way she wants people to know it. She's the ultimate media manipulator.

She embraces confrontation and discomfort

When questioned by anyone, she'll take a considered pause before choosing how to respond. This means she's never hurried, never out of control or rushed into reacting. How she operates is on her terms, at all times. She'll ask others difficult questions and stay silent while they squirm to find an answer. Whilst they do this she silently scans them for signs of weakness that inform her follow up questions and her next actions. She'll find out exactly what she needs to know whilst giving away the least information possible herself. She'll let others fill the silences so they say too much. She'll let others make interpretations that lead them to the wrong conclusions.

Everything here combines to give Claire even more of the power she is looking for. No one can shock her, no one can hurt her, no one can hold anything over her and she'll never face a situation whereby she doesn't know what to do next. Claire is a truly intriguing character. If you look past the moral and legal wrongdoings, of which there are many, we could all do with being just that bit more Claire Underwood.

"I'm just so fundamentally optimistic, and I barrel forth in life with this attitude that everything is going to be absolutely fine and go my way."

Amanda Palmer

No One Cares About Your Problems, So Make It Look Easy

I saw a postcard in Berlin that read: "Some people have real problems".

Whatever you think is going wrong, whatever problems you think you have, someone always has it worse. I promise you. There are people fighting aggressive illnesses in hospital, people living without clean water, in places of war. Yes, it's all relative, but you must have perspective.

So if your problems are small in comparison, why do you feel compelled to share them online?

On the surface, venting on social media might seem harmless. You're human, right? You feel people should know you're going through a really hard time or that you've suffered an injustice. But why do you need the validation? Are you looking for sympathy? Or just some attention?

Plenty of research shows that sharing and talking through your problems is beneficial to your mental health. Here's where you need to cultivate your inner circle of trust. Your best friends. People you admire and respect and who you can trust with anything. This circle is smaller than you think. It's definitely not all of your Twitter followers.

In reality, the effect of publicising your problems is truly detrimental to the success you are trying to achieve.

In ranting, complaining and making backhanded or snide comments you will look like you have no control. You look like you have no power over your own destiny, that you have no plan, and that life just happens to you and you moan about it.

In the short term, people will think of you either as someone who makes bad decisions, has a lot of bad luck, or who loves pointless drama. In the long term, you will drain people and they will avoid you. You will come across like you settle for average, blame other people, divert things and explain them away instead of taking control and taking action.

It's ok not to have all the answers, it's ok to go through a rough time, but you don't need to promote that fact. This is your personal brand, so control it! You can share all the tough times you went through after you've made it, you don't need to dwell on it until them.

Posting backhanded comments on social media? Shame on you for not sorting out your own situation sooner. Other people are not responsible for your happiness. At best, your posts will evoke a small degree of empathy. At worst they look utterly pathetic. Everyone knows there are two sides to every story. What does sharing yours achieve?

Think everyone else has it easy? I constantly meet business owners who are convinced there are easier ways of making money than how they're currently doing it. They've met people running other business who seem to have it so good. It must just be that they chose a better market, a better business model or were more fortunate with their timing. Really? Or what if they just haven't broadcasted their problems?

In my experience, there are no easy businesses. I'm part of a network called Dynamite Circle, location-independent entrepreneurs running all sorts of companies. Some of them own "lifestyle businesses" which might appear to be blogging from a beach but actually involve a hell of a lot of trial, error, algorithm changes, app updates and tariff surfing. It's easy to develop a major case of *grass is always greener* syndrome. However easy someone else seems to have it; everyone has problems.

The title of the Hemingway novel, The Sun Also Rises, depicts the potential for optimism in the perpetual rising of the run. In a similar vein, Ecclesiastes 1:5 includes the phrase "The sun also ariseth, and the sun goeth down, and hasteth to his place where he arose." Both are about the cycles of the world and how they happen every day.

You're not the first one to face the problem you are facing and you won't be the first one to solve it. Broadly speaking, everyone has similar trials and tribulations throughout their working life. Things will always crop up so you might as well be good at dealing with them.

There are two types of person. The former, who dramatises everything that happens to them and make it everyone else's problem and the latter, who makes it look easy.

I recently interviewed executive leadership coach Oona Collins, who works with high-performing executives or business leaders in the public eye. I was fascinated with Oona explaining that there can be huge strength in vulnerability. However, she was careful to emphasise that for vulnerability to be a strength it needs to be well timed, purposeful and infrequent. It's a tool to use when you really need to use it, not as part of your day-to-day.

In Robert Greene's best-selling book, the 48 Laws of Power, law of power number 30 is "Make it look easy". It's my favourite one.

Don't share every single aspect of the journey you're on, there's no point, for all the reasons I've mentioned. Communicate the right information, to the right people, at the right time. Share things when they are signed, sealed delivered, not before. No one needs to know the detail; your entire network doesn't need to know about your problems.

Don't become known for being all about the talk and nothing about the substance. Get your head down and put the work in. Share the fruits of your labour, not the labour itself. You will appear superhuman. Make it look easy.

"I've met many small business owners, founders, and entrepreneurs in my time. I feel the most long-standing ones possess three things: positive mindset, resilient approach, and they treat others as they would like to be treated themselves. It's so sad when you see the opposite."

Emma Jones MBE

How Entrepreneurs Can Be Bulletproof

As an entrepreneur, you put yourself in the firing line every day. You know full well that bad things will happen. You will be shot at.

Staff will move on, clients will leave. Competitors will compete. Haters will hate. You do everything in your power to mitigate the risk of these things happening, but some events are just out of your control. You come to appreciate that this is what your role entails. It's not a case of trying to dodge the bullets; it's a case of becoming bulletproof. This is why resilience and a sense of invincibility are fundamental to your existence.

But just knowing and accepting that adverse circumstances will occur doesn't make you bulletproof.

When world-class sports people compete under huge pressure in make-or-break moments in their career, they have practiced what they are about to do thousands of times before. They give themselves every chance of succeeding, whatever the game throws at them.

As a business owner, many of the situations you find yourself in are brand new. This means you are regularly reacting to high-pressure, critical situations and being forced to think on your feet. Things will change. People will present you problems. Deadlines will be missed. Here's where you really find out if you are bulletproof. Are you able to make the right decisions and move forward without creating unnecessary drama and your mood, demeanour or outlook being negatively affected?

If you are overly emotional and in the wrong frame of mine you will make bad decisions that could have long-term implications for your business.

"Everyone has a plan until they get punched in the face."

- Mike Tyson

In the Ben Horowitz book, The Hard Thing About Hard Things, Horowitz explains:

"The hard thing isn't setting big, audacious goals. The hard thing is laying people off when you miss the big goals."

Running a business is easy when everything is on track. You only find out if you're bulletproof when the wheels fall off.

I believe that negative visualisation should play a key role in how modern entrepreneurs operate. Rather than visualising your success, achievements and dream lifestyle, negative visualisation involves visualising yourself in various adverse scenarios - challenging you to consider your emotional response and next moves.

Of course, you cannot possibly have dress rehearsals for every eventuality in your business, but you can better equip yourself for when they happen. A phrase I always bear in mind is, "Expect the best, prepare for the worst".

The Daily Stoic reports on a technique called a premortem, designed by psychologist Gary Klein and with roots in Stoic philosophy, whereby a project manager must envision what could go wrong, what *will* go wrong, in advance, before starting a project. They go on to explain:

"Far too many people don't have a backup plan because they refuse to consider that something might not go exactly as they wish."

Consider the three worst things that could possibly happen to you and your business. Accept that these are all potential realities and imagine that each one had actually happened. Place yourself there. Imagine what it is like to receive this news. How do you feel? What's your instinctive reaction? Then, consider the next five steps you'd take to deal with this situation and move forward positively.

No matter how bad the situation, there is always a course of action you can take. In doing this exercise you might get to thinking that these worse case scenarios aren't actually that bad, and even that some of them would have benefits for your business in the long run.

I practice negative visualisation regularly and find that the best time to do it is when things are going well. Expect the best, prepare for the worst. Consider that if you can deal with the absolute worse case scenario, you can deal with anything.

Once you have full confidence in your own ability, once you can genuinely say you back yourself to deal with whatever is thrown at you, and to thrive regardless of any adversity, that's when you will feel invincible and on the way to becoming bulletproof.

"Where one person sees a crisis, another can see opportunity. Where one is blinded by success, another sees reality with ruthless objectivity. Where one loses control of emotions, another can remain calm."

Ryan Holiday

How
To
Be
Happy
(Nearly)
All
The
Time

In the illustrated book, Brave Girls Club, Melody Ross describes happiness as, quite simply, "a choice that we make every minute of every day". Happiness is a much researched and sought-after state of being that philosophers and great thinkers alike have tried to explain. As they see it - happiness is simple and achievable.

When you're faced with transition, change and disruption, happiness can feel unobtainable. I believe it's there to be found, but not in the way you might believe it can be. Here's my take on happiness: reimagined, with 9 somewhat unconventional ways to be happy (nearly) all the time.

1. Love people; use things.

The 2015 documentary The Minimalists follows the journey of Joshua Fields Millburn and Ryan Nicodemus defining the actual important aspects of life. Their mantra? "Love people, use things. The opposite never works." Got an urge for something shiny? Keep asking why. Why do I want to buy that car? Because it will make me look successful. Why do I care about looking successful? Because of what [person] will think. Why do I care what [person] thinks? Well? Hang out with people who don't care what car you drive, because it really doesn't matter.

If we don't find the way to happiness ourselves, other people will tell us how to get there. Marketing teaches you what not to be happy with: our relationships, job or appearance. Advertising guides us towards specific goods and services on the premise that they'll make us happy. In reality, people often find that the things that they think will make them happy actually don't. Money. Fame. Possessions. It's well documented that lottery winners often regret having ever won the money.

Day-to-day this means focusing on the time you can spend with people you love and not on the objects you can purchase. Gifting your presence instead of buying presents. Avoid those who make you feel rubbish and go see those who you enjoy spending time with.

2. Get some perspective.

In the Derren Brown book, Happy: Why More or Less Everything is Absolutely Fine, Brown says "Everything worthwhile in your life draws its meaning from the fact you will die." The Stoics use the Latin phrase "memento mori" as their reminder of mortality.

Get comfortable with the idea that one day you and everyone you know won't be here. Let that dictate your every moment. Find happiness in the absurdity that we're all taking ourselves so seriously when really it doesn't even matter. Wicked: The Musical describes it best in their song Dancing Through Life, with the lyrics "Nothing matters, but knowing nothing matters." That person who slagged you off behind your back? Who cares?! That competitor who copies everything you do. So what?! Good luck to them all. You hope they make it. It's not a zero sum game and thinking it is ignores the real heart of the matter - you're not going to live forever.

Find freedom in the fact that whatever happens, one day you'll be gone, so you might as well be happy today while you are alive. Your problems really aren't that big.

Not only are your problems not that big, you're not the first person to go through what you're going through and you won't be the last. There's comfort and happiness in knowing that people have gone before you and solved the problems you are solving right now. It can be done, and you can do it, so smile.

3. Control the controllables.

Herbert Bayard Swope once said "I can't give you a sure-fire formula for success, but I can give you a formula for failure: try to please everybody all the time." Now I'm not promising I can give you a formula for happiness, but a definite formula for unhappiness is to worry and stress about things that are completely out of your control.

In season 5 episode 18 of US sitcom Friends, Monica is throwing a party and wants to control everything: the food, the guest list and the entertainment. Phoebe tries to help and Monica, to keep her away, puts her in charge of two things that she deems insignificant: cups and ice. Phoebe is now clear that most of the party is out of her control, but she goes to town on what she can control: cups and ice. She makes cup bunting, cup towers, ice sculptures, snow cones, dry ice, crushed, cubed, and so on. She promises that Monica will "rue the day she put [her] in charge of cups and ice". The cups and ice become the centrepiece and the talking points of the entire gathering, much to Monica's annoyance.

The first step is to work out what is in your control and what is out of your control. Other people's actions? Out of your control. The football score? Out of your control. What people think? Out of your control. In your control: your attitude, your actions, your words, your thoughts, your choices. Make a list. Focus on what you can control and give it everything you have. Forget everything else.

4. Avoid labels.

When something happens it's human nature to want to define it. It's "awesome", it's "bad", it's "unfair". Actually, it's none of those things; it's just something that has happened. The label given to it is purely one person's perspective, not necessarily the truth.

When I was on my graduate scheme, my manager Glynn was from Sheffield and spoke in idioms. One day he used the line, "At the end of the day, it is what it is and that's that." At the time I thought that phrase was a convoluted way of saying absolutely nothing. Now I realise it was deeply profound. At the end of the day it is what it is and that's that. I have since found that training my brain to see things as they are, and avoiding the perceptions and labels that can surround them, has avoided drama and headaches like nothing else. Go one step further by avoiding the need to hear other people's opinions. Opinion pieces on current political happenings, what [outspoken celebrity] thinks about what [another celebrity] has said or done. Who cares, right? Avoid forming opinions, because opinions don't make you happy.

Start avoiding opinions day-to-day and you will realise how often they are aired. Opinions are just that; they are not the truth so never treat them as such. Like a ball being thrown at you; you choose whether to catch it or dodge it. You don't need to disagree (that would be an opinion too), just be mindful of what you choose to let enter your inner being. Your thoughts become your words and your words become your actions, and, by extension, your reputation and success.

"We are, each of us, a product of the stories we tell ourselves"

- Derren Brown

5. It's all a game.

In his bestselling book, Key Person of Influence, Daniel Priestly says "The minute you begin to feel yourself "working hard" as opposed to "playing a challenging game," it's time to take a break." I believe that given everything in point (3), happiness comes from viewing everything as playing a challenging game. Not just work but life too.

Accept that things out of your control will happen and they won't all be favourable. You must be ready for them. Taking a break in the short term might help, but in the long term, train yourself to deal with anything that comes at you. Because it will keep coming at you and it won't stop, so you might as well get good at it.

Whilst you might crave picturesque scenery, rolling hills and nothing but the sound of birds singing, real happiness comes from calmness in the middle of a crowd, in the middle of a tense conversation or on the battlefield. Happiness is riding the waves and not being pulled about with each occurrence like an emotional rollercoaster.

A technique I learned about in the Tim Ferriss book, Tools of Titans, is saying the word "good" after anything that happens. Anything. My work got deleted? Good. A chance to do it again, better. The internet is down? Good. A chance to read a book. My food is taking ages to arrive? Good. A chance to practice patience. I feel overwhelmed? Good. A chance to make a change. Doing this conditions your brain to see opportunities rather than problems in every set of circumstances.

6. Don't take it personally

In Confessions of a Conjuror, Derren Brown writes: "Each of us is leading a difficult life, and when we meet people we are seeing only a tiny part of the thinnest veneer of their complex, troubled existences. To practise anything other than kindness towards them, to treat them in any way save generously, is to quietly deny their humanity."

It would be easy to let the actions of others dictate your happiness, but what would this achieve? If you receive an email you perceive to be unfriendly, or someone cuts you up, or doesn't let you out, it's not personal. That person might have just lost a family member, they might be dealing with problems far worse than yours. They probably didn't mean it to upset you. Seeing other people and their actions as being out to get you is the sure fire route to unhappiness, because in reality it's probably nothing to do with you.

There's a bias that can happen when individuals assess their own and others' behaviour: attribution bias. According to Wikipedia, when judging others we tend to assume their actions are the result of internal factors such as their personality, whereas we tend to assume our own actions arise because of the necessity of external circumstances. So when someone turns up late to a meeting with you, you might label them as lazy or inconsiderate, but they will explain their lateness by pointing to the traffic jam or train timetable. Happiness is being able to understand the actions of others, not label their character.

Judging the character of others or taking everything personally happens when you can only see your side of the story. Seeing the other side of the story requires empathising. You don't need to go into problem solving mode on someone else's life. See point (4) and control what you can control. The label you give it, your response, keeping your cool. It's not about you.

7. Do the right thing, even if it's hard

"The right way is not always the popular and easy way. Standing for what is right when it is unpopular is a true test of moral character."

- Margaret C.S.

There's often a difference between what is easy and what is right. Doing what is easy is... well... easy. Choosing the easy option means you don't call a team member up for poor performance because you don't want a difficult conversation; it's easier to make excuses for them or do the work yourself. You don't send back the food you've been served even though it's not what you ordered; it's easier to just eat it. Doing the easy thing instead of the right thing might seem like a path to happiness, but it's short-sighted and only works in the short term. In the long term, doing the right thing lays far better foundations, for your work, relationships and mindset.

Joel Runyon of Impossible X advises going one step further, by actively seeking out the hard things, to embrace them and overcome them. The happiness is found in realising that the hard thing was within your ability to solve.

How do you decide what is the right thing? How do you tackle the hard things? Go back to your morals, values, and just being a decent human being, whilst having a commitment to excellence and being exceptional.

Similarly, the Dalai Lama XIV explains the following in The Art of Happiness: "The more honest you are, the more open, the less fear you will have, because there's no anxiety about being exposed or revealed to others."

If you always do the right thing, even if it's difficult, and stay true to your values, you will never worry about anyone's opinion of you, you will never need to look over your shoulder, and you will sleep soundly. Happiness all round.

8. Subtract

This concept is taken from a blog post by Derek Sivers, where he explains that the world pushes us to add and keep adding, but actually life can be improved by subtracting. Here, Sivers talks about successful people, but I think this applies to happiness too:

"The least successful people I know run in conflicting directions, drawn to distractions, say yes to almost everything, and are chained to emotional obstacles."

"The most successful people I know have a narrow focus, protect against time-wasters, say no to almost everything, and have let go of old limiting beliefs."

In practice, you can take a piece of paper and split it into four. At the top of each section write these headings: Start, stop, more, less. Then write down those things you want start, stop, do more of and do less of. Begin with 'stop' and 'less'. Stop scrolling Instagram. Stop reacting to sensationalised headlines. Less fulfilling obligations you don't want to. Less sitting in traffic. Less rushing. Fewer meetings. And so on.

Then you can move on to 'start' and 'more', with a new sense of clarity and space. In The Happiness Project, Gretchen Rubin links freeing up space to giving yourself better options, where she explains "I can DO ANYTHING I want, but I can't DO EVERYTHING I want."

Adapt your thinking so that you see blank space in your diary as a chance to reflect and get into deep work that really makes a difference or furthers your cause. Adapt your thinking so that a clean and clear room means clarity and space, not bare or un-homely. You don't need to; as Seneca puts it in his essays, On The Shortness of Life, "hurry about town fulfilling pointless social obligations".

You simply cannot best serve the needs of your company, family or friends without serving your own needs first. You can't look after other people if you don't look after yourself. Guard your diary fiercely and decide what goes into your metaphorical backpack. Avoid being so busy you never get to enjoy yourself.

9. Be present.

There are two sides to this point. The first is about your mind and body being present in any situation, rather than your body being there but your mind being somewhere else.

Hedging between watching the fireworks and filming them on your phone isn't happiness. Meeting a friend for dinner whilst worrying about tomorrow's day at work isn't happiness. At best you'll appear distant and vacant. At worst you'll lose a friend. Happiness is giving your complete undivided attention to given situation that you have chosen to be in. If you don't want to be there, opt out all together. If you decide to show up, give it the energy it warrants.

The second side to this point is about being firmly in the present, not the past or the future. Seneca puts it best:

"True happiness is to enjoy the present, without anxious dependence upon the future, not to amuse ourselves with either hopes or fears but to rest satisfied with what we have, which is sufficient, for he that is so wants nothing. The greatest blessings of mankind are within us and within our reach. A wise man is content with his lot, whatever it may be, without wishing for what he has not."

In the book Stumbling on Happiness by Daniel Gilbert, he says, "The human being is the only animal that thinks about the future." Worrying about what the future might bring isn't happiness. Plan for the future, sure, but focus it on the actions that you can implement in the present. Revisiting conversations held in the past and reciting the better answers you could have given isn't happiness. Let it go.

Also from the Happiness Project, Rubin explains, "When I find myself focusing overmuch on the anticipated future happiness of arriving at a certain goal, I remind myself to "Enjoy now". If I can enjoy the present, I don't need to count on the happiness that is (or isn't) waiting for me in the future."

Being present is key to happiness because the present is the only aspect of time that's in your control. There's nothing you can do about the past. Worrying about bad things that might happen in the future means you're either wasting your time (if they don't happen) or suffering twice (if they do). Being somewhere with your body whilst your mind is elsewhere means you might as well not be there. This also links back to point two: 'get some perspective'. One day you won't be here. Today might be your last day on earth. Might as well be present while you can.

True happiness comes from knowing what is in your control and out of your control and acting accordingly, whilst being careful what you let into your inner sphere.

It's doing the right thing, even if it's hard. True happiness is found when you look to subtract rather than add, and when you are firmly in the present at all times

It comes from watching your thoughts for those that are unhelpful or untrue, showing kindness wherever possible and, above everything else, remembering it's all a game and we're not going to live forever.

"The next Michelangelo could be sitting behind a MacBook right now writing an invoice for paperclips, because it pays the bills, or because it is comfortable, or because he can tolerate it."

Bianca Sparacino

There's Only One Way To Succeed

After 8 years of running my own agency, working with many clients, colleagues and suppliers, it's now clear to me what separates those individuals who are remarkable, impressive and – ultimately – successful from those who are replaceable and forgettable.

"You're either remarkable or invisible. Make a choice."

- Seth Godin

I've written before about the difference between doing what is right and what is easy, and the importance of committing to excellence no matter what. Having researched and been fascinated by the right versus easy theory, and taken inspiration from authors in this field, I now believe it's more fundamental to success than we realise. The right thing to do is often the hardest. The one most avoided. The one that's carried forward to next week or deemed too tricky. But it's the most important by a long way.

Ben Horowitz commits a whole book to describing and defining the Hard Thing About Hard Things. Cal Newport wrote Digital Minimalism and Deep Work to distinguish between the easy distractions that technology offer versus the, sometimes seemingly unattainable, deep and focused effort that makes the real difference. The 48 Laws of Power by Robert Greene includes rules on outsmarting, outworking and outlasting rivals, albeit whilst making it look easy.

This isn't about seeking difficulty for no reason. This isn't about being abrasive or argumentative when there's just no need to (and rarely is there a need to!). This is about knowing what to let slide and what to address, knowing the difference between a short cut that's beneficial and one that defers problems only in the short term. It's about knowing when your opinion is welcome and when you have no place offering it.

Let's start with the easy things. When running a business, the easy things are great, and include the following: hiring great people who get off to flying starts and are eager to please. Giving praise, giving pay rises, sharing good vibes. It's easy to share good news before it's fully confirmed, to paint a rosy picture of the future and sell it to your board, shareholders or team. It's easy to take your clients for a drink, get to know them well and make small talk. It's easy to talk to people about your ambitious growth plans. In any role, it's easy to talk; to give away more information than required, to gossip about co-workers, to criticise the actions of others and think you know best. It's easy to read a headline and jump to a conclusion, or fly off the handle at a snippet of information.

However, without the hard things that accompany all of these easy things, you'll build a business with little substance. It will be superficial, shallow, and won't stand up to stress tests, like a house of cards ready to collapse.

Be wary of hiring managers who are great at doing the easy things but don't have the experience, commercial awareness or authority to do the hard things, and don't fall into the trap yourself.

The hard things are those that I believe are prioritised, executed and even enjoyed by those entrepreneurs and business leaders who really do stand out as being exceptional at what they do. They include: Working out their own weaknesses and addressing them without relying on others. Having the difficult yet necessary conversations to give the feedback or constructive criticism that someone needs to hear in order to improve and progress. Doing the most important thing on their to-do list first, always. Picking up the phone instead of hiding behind email or assistants. Revisiting a strategy for the fifth time to ensure the best results possible. Knowing when enough is enough and having the strength to back down, cut their losses or say goodbye.

It's not easy to pull the wall down and rebuild it instead of papering over the cracks. It takes courage to refuse to participate in gossip, rumour or biased opinions. Always seeing the other side of the story and withholding judgment until you have all of the information requires practice, as does verifying before trusting implicitly. You might not enjoy empathising with someone you really don't like, or showing kindness that has no chance of reciprocation, but do it anyway. Above all, the hardest thing to do is to always, without fail, back yourself to thrive and survive in any given set of circumstances. Which, funnily enough, is only possible when you're truly committed to doing what is right, even when it's difficult.

"Those who say it cannot be done should not interrupt those who are doing it."

- Unknown

Shying away from impactful and meaningful actions that really move the needle in favour of shallow niceties and fluffy stuff is harming your career and stunting your business. I'm certain that, deep down, everyone knows when they are doing something worthwhile and when they are just passing the time to little avail. Let this be the sign that it's time to do the former.

"Believe whatever you need to believe
to do your best work."

Sahil Lavingia

How
It
Feels
When
You Have
Nothing
To
Prove

When you have nothing to prove your only competition is your former self. You carry out actions because you believe them to be the right thing to do, which is enough. You find it easy to show kindness and you seek no reward in return. You hold no grudges. You seek no revenge. You forgive anyone who has attempted to hurt you or who wishes you harm. You feel sad that others waste their time and energy proving themselves or justifying their actions but you hope they find happiness regardless. You look forward to the day when they feel how you do, because it feels peaceful and calm.

You let everything slide like never before. No one's words can touch you. They only serve to make you smile. You keep your head down and you do your work. You continue with your cause and you make progress. What you're working on is bigger and more important. Titles and awards are nice, but that's not what you're doing it for. You find success in your input, not the output you can't control. You would never diss anyone on the internet. You don't need to. You know your time on earth is finite, the same as everyone else's, so we might as well happily co-exist together.

You cultivate the friendships that mean the most to you and you accept that you won't click with everyone you meet. You don't need to be liked or understood. Anyone worth it will ask. No one worth it will make judgments based on second hand information. Nothing can touch you because you're firmly in the driving seat of your own life, not a spectator in someone else's.

Let this be the year you truly have nothing to prove to anyone but yourself. Be your own best friend, biggest fan and harshest critic. If something or someone doesn't add to your life, forget they exist and move on. You have nothing to prove and you never will.

"Things can only get better, or worse, or stay pretty much the same, and we look forward to it."

Howard of Warwick

The
Alternative
Ways
To
Be
Rich

You can be rich the traditional way. You can have cash in the bank, assets to your name and income rolling in. You can buy whatever you want, whenever you want it. You can hire people to do chores for you and you can drive around in flashy wheels. Whatever you desire, you can purchase. You are rich because you have everything you want.

But it's not that simple. As quoted in Fight Club, "The things you own end up owning you." Owning a nice big house isn't as fun when you're worrying about being broken into. Owning expensive clothes stop you playing games with your nieces and nephews, a nice garden needs hours of upkeep, fancy sunglasses get sat on.

From the Daily Stoic, "Income taxes are not the only taxes you pay in life. They are just the financial form. Everything we do has a toll attached to it. Waiting around is a tax on traveling. Rumours and gossip are the taxes that come from acquiring a public persona. Disagreements and occasional frustration are taxes placed on even the happiest of relationships. Theft is a tax on abundance and having things that other people want."

This doesn't mean you shouldn't strive for success and riches, but take the taxes into account, or learn to see past them. Put it into perspective. Would you rather focus on what you get to keep or what you have to give away?

There's having everything you want, and then there's having nothing you don't want. Achieving the latter could change things for you right now. Those who are truly wealthy have enough, and this is sufficient. They don't long for more. So being rich is not only about financial status or material ownership but freedom from burdens; things you don't want or need in your life.

This isn't about ticking milestones off your to-do list; this is about defining your "not-to-do" list. Identify the people, the possessions and the obligations that you just don't want to be part of your existence and say no to them. Say no to drama, negativity and naysayers. Say no to that huge teddy from the theme park, or that family heirloom you don't actually like. Free up time, room and headspace for experiences and possessions that really spark joy. Cultivate deeper relationships with your few favourite people instead of having arms-length small talk with hundreds. If you really hate doing something, work out how you can take it out of your equation. Focus on eliminating everything at the bottom of your list alongside maximising the top. Feel like a millionaire without actually being one.

Richness comes from the elevated quality of every hour you have, so another way of being rich is having autonomy over how you spend your time. That includes: Waking up when you want to. Having time to read books, time to exercise and a short commute. Time to spend with friends but the freedom to write or work all night if you want to do that, too. There's happiness in having the choice of whom you spend time with and whom you choose to let go, at work and at home. Having ultimate mastery over your days, weeks and years might be more attractive than being at the beck and call of a thousand customers. What's the trade-off you're willing to make, and how can you have the best of both worlds?

"There's always a gap between "what I have now" and "what I would like." And that gap is all of your excuses."

James Altucher

Take Control Of Your Own Happiness

If you are relying on anyone or anything else for your happiness, stop that right now. If you feel like you're not quite doing what you want to be doing and you're not quite the person you want to be, let reading this be the sign that you have a change to make.

There are those who take control of their life and there are those who are life's victims. Which do you want to be? The type who confidently assesses their own worth or the type that complains about feeling undervalued? No one can make you feel anything. Happy or sad. Every emotion you feel, you can be in charge of. Giving away control of your feelings? Get a grip.

Here are 6 ways to create and control your own happiness:

1. Evaluate yourself

Be prepared to give yourself honest and ruthless feedback and don't forget to learn each time you mess up. If you've already assessed and addressed your own weaknesses, what can anyone else's opinion matter? Get comfortable with your strengths – look for opportunities to use them. Nothing you hear in a formal appraisal or passing comment should surprise you. Don't rely on others to point out your shortcomings.

2. Make a change

If you always do what you've always done, you'll always get what you've always got. If you always avoid difficult conversations, you'll always work with a team that isn't up to scratch. If you always blame others, you'll never take ownership and you'll never be the best you can be.

Everything that happens is a cyclical process that will continue until you make an intervention - a change that puts you on a new course. Happy where every part of your life is going? Great! Go you! More of the same. Feel like you're missing something? Make a change. Somewhere. If what you're putting out there isn't working, or isn't manifesting the results you want, it's only you that can get you back on the way to happy.

3. Stop comparing

It happens all the time. You're happy with your job until you hear about someone else's and it sounds much better. You're happy with the growth of your business until you hear of someone else's growing faster. You feel like things are going pretty well until a peer does something you'd love to do. If you compare your life to anything other than a former version of itself, you're asking for unhappiness. Even some of the most successful and inspiring people I know have moments where they want to swap places with someone else. It's madness. Sure, there are other things you could be doing, but choosing to do them would mean forgoing your current path. Keep forgoing your current path and you'll end up flitting around with no agenda, copying the last success story you read on the internet. Make comparisons with no one but your former self.

4. Define happiness

Ever seen the BBC show Saturday Kitchen? Each episode, James Martin, the presenter, cooks one of two dishes for the special guest - their *food heaven* or their *food hell*. My food hell is a seafood linguine with some kind of pea, mint and fennel sauce. Every part of that dish absolutely disgusts me. Yuck. I know, however, that the dish I've described will be someone else's *food heaven*. Life and work are the same. The choices you make and the reality you live will be someone else's version of hell, and vice versa. So the happiness you seek has to be based on your version of happiness and not someone else's. Definitely not based on TV adverts, celebrity Instagram pictures or the lives of friends and relatives.

5. Keep your lips sealed

Work out your own plan before you ask for comment. Be sure of your next move before you open up to receive advice. Recognise that every time you share your intentions you leave yourself susceptible to be influenced. Get clear on your plan, put the work in, then share the results, not the journey.

6. Design your life

In the 4-Hour Work Week, by Tim Ferriss, he advises an exercise where you take a piece of paper and write down: Every day, every other day, every week, every month, every quarter, every year. You then write down the things you'd like to do in those frequencies. They could be "go for a walk" every day. "Have a meal with friends" every week, "Go to Disneyland" every year. Anything you like! Try it out. Write them all down and use that piece of paper as a blueprint for living a life full of your favourite things.

If you can't define what makes you happy then you will forever be confused as to how you achieve it. If you can define it exactly, no amount of Insta-envy or assessments from others will touch you. Accept that what you've just written down will be someone else's version of hell, and plough on regardless!

Only you have the power and inclination to control your own happiness. No external factors should penetrate your inner core. You've got this!

"When I'm old, how much would I be willing to pay to travel back in time and relive the moment that I'm experiencing right now?"

Muneeb Ali

About the author

Since starting her social media agency in 2011 Jodie has been fascinated by the influences that create entrepreneurs.

She co-wrote a series of children's storybooks, Clever Tykes, which develop positive, resourceful and creative behaviour in 6-9 year olds; they are now read in every primary school in the United Kingdom and she's determined to replicate this in countries across the world.

Jodie was included in Forbes' 30 under 30 social entrepreneurs in Europe 2017 and gave a TEDx talk with the title 'creating useful people'.

She's big on travel, lifestyle design and helping people access the freedom that entrepreneurship should bring.

Jodie writes books and articles on happiness, entrepreneurship and social media.

jodiecook.com/books
Twitter: @cookiewhirls

Printed in Great Britain
by Amazon